The PEPPERMINT BARK COOKBOOK

The PEPPERMINT BARK COOKBOOK

Over 75 Recipes for Delicious Homemade Treats, from Milkshakes to Cheesecakes

DOMINIQUE DEVITO

CIDER MILL PRESS

BOOK PUBLISHERS

KENNEBUNKPORT, MAINE

13-Digit ISBN: 9781604336719
10-Digit ISBN: 1604336714

This book may be ordered by mail from the publisher. Please include $5.95 foar postage and handling. Please support your local bookseller first!

Books published by Cider Mill Press Book Publishers are available at special discounts for bulk purchases in the United States by corporations, institutions, and other organizations. For more information, please contact the publisher.

Cider Mill Press Book Publishers
"Where good books are ready for press"
PO Box 454
12 Spring Street
Kennebunkport, Maine 04046

Visit us on the Web!
www.cidermillpress.com

Cover design by Melissa Gerber

Interior design by Alicia Freile, Tango Media

Typography: Baker Street, Bell MT, Copperplate, LHF Billhead, LHF Noel's Thes, Lobster Two, Microbrew

Image on page 60 used under license from iStock/(c)StanleyPhotography
Image on page 114 used under license from iStock/(c)~User44956e1d_22
Image on page 154 used under license from iStock/(c)Magone
Image on page 174 used under license from iStock/(c)TravisLincoln
Image on page 206 used under license from iStock/(c)Taylor Hinton
Image on page 27 courtesy of Dominique Devito
All other photos used under official license from Shutterstock.com.

Printed in China

2 3 4 5 6 7 8 9 0

To the sweetest guys I know: Dawson and Dylan.
I'll bark about you and with you any day.

CONTENTS

Welcome to the World of Bark

Peppermint bark is one of life's true simple pleasures. It's beautiful to look at and makes you want to smile. And it's great to give as gifts because it looks great, tastes amazing, and is really easy to make!

So without further ado, let's get you started on your peppermint bark journey. This book is loaded with variations on peppermint bark (which of course needs to include peppermint), and also has recipes for barks featuring everything from nuts to coconut to cookies and even bacon and cayenne pepper! There are recipes for other desserts and snacks to make that have peppermint bark in them, like traditional brownies and cheesecake, and even potato chips and popcorn. There are recipes for chocolate treats other than bark, and—yes!—there are recipes for bark-inspired beverages!!

First, though, there are some things you need to consider before getting started, and they're mostly about chocolate, so it's easy (and important) to pay attention. They are:

- What is chocolate exactly?
- Understanding the differences in chocolate
- Baking with chocolate
- Proper melting of chocolate
- Proper storage of chocolate
- Parchment vs. waxed paper

Chocolate's Roots—Er, Seeds

The journey from earth to eaten for chocolate starts in the cacao tree, whose Latin name, *Theobroma cacao*, translates to "food of the gods." The tree produces pods and seeds. The pods are opened and fermented, then the seeds are dried, roasted, and tempered to produce the components of edible chocolate— now called cocoa—which are butter, powder, and liquor.

Cacao trees are believed to have originated east of the Andes in South America, though an exact origin isn't known. As their pods and seeds became popular, they spread into the upper Amazon and into Central America and Mexico. Eventually, sub-species developed—the criollo in Central America and the forastero in South America. There are endless debates and discussions about the flavor and quality differences.

For connoisseurs of chocolate, the stuff is as multi-layered as wine. There are actually over 600 volatile compounds that contribute to chocolate's aromas and flavors, and they have to do with the variety of the tree, the place where it's grown, how the fermentation is done, and then how it is dried, roasted, and tempered. And that gives you just the base product. From there, flavor and texture enhancers are added, including sugars and fats.

For most of the time that it's been ingested by humans (dating back several thousand years BC), cocoa was a bitter drink. Even in this form, it was believed to have magical properties, not the least of which was as a potent aphrodisiac.

COCOA-LOCO

The "cocoa" we know as chocolate today is called that because it's the product of the cacao tree, typically considered the powdered version, whereas chocolate is the solid version. It was the Spaniards who decided the elixir needed sweetening after it was presented to them by the Aztecs in the 1500s and they deemed it too bitter. Cacao became a prized commodity in Europe, where it remained a beverage for the upper classes only. It wasn't until the early 1800s that a chemist figured out how to remove some natural fat (cacao butter) from the chocolate "liquor" (liquid), pulverize the powder, and add alkaline to further reduce the bitter taste. His "Dutch cocoa" was the predecessor of solid chocolate. It wasn't long after that the candy bar was invented, commercialization was applied to chocolate production, and chocolate became available for—and eagerly consumed by—the general public.

The Mayans sipped it during their most important ceremonies, including betrothal and marriage. It was so valued that it was a delicacy for kings and the upper classes only, and pods were traded as currency.

Cacao played a large part in medicine, too. Brews containing it were made to treat everything from infections to coughs, to gout, hemorrhoids, rashes, seizures, and even dental problems. When the production and consumption of cacao came to Europe, doctors were as eager to experiment with it as confectioners. A treatise from 1631 cites Spanish physician, Antonio Colmenero de Ledesma, praising cacao's medicinal properties: "It quite takes away the Morpheus, cleaneth the teeth, and sweeteneth the breath, provokes urine, cures the stones, and expels poison, and preserves from all infectious diseases."

Dark, White, and In-Between

Chocolate isn't as simple as suspected, is it? If you bake with chocolate already, or have made chocolate confections, you know that there are several kinds of chocolates to work with. It gets confusing, but once your palette comes into play, you'll discover which chocolates are most enjoyable for you.

Choosing Chocolate

For the recipes in this book, I've chosen to keep the chocolate selection relatively simple. Semi-sweet is most often called for, especially when it's being combined with white chocolate, which is sweeter. Semi-sweet chocolate is readily available in bars and chips. For white chocolate, I recommend using bars as the quality tends to be better than the chips, but chips can be a fine substitute. Fortunately, chocolate for baking is now available in morsels and bars, and dark, semi-sweet, milk, and white chocolates are easy to find.

Bittersweet, Dark, and Semi-Sweet

Chocolates that are labeled with these designations must contain at least 35% unsweetened chocolate and can only contain up to 12% milk solids. There are dark chocolates that are labeled as up to 90% cocoa, and semi-sweet with over 35%. The standard percentage of cacao in semi-sweet chocolate is 35 to 45% cacao. In dark chocolate, which is also "bittersweet," the percentage is usually 50 to 75%. The highest concentration of cacao in solid form is 100%, and that is unsweetened chocolate. It has no sugar.

Milk Chocolate

As its name suggests, it's dairy solids that give milk chocolate its name. These are combined with the base of at least 10% cacao and 12% milk solids. Other ingredients are cream and sugar in varying amounts.

White Chocolate

Interestingly, white chocolate—which contains no chocolate "liquor" (from which cacao is processed)—does contain cocoa butter, another of the resultant ingredients from cacao production. Products labeled as white chocolate must contain at least 20% cocoa butter and 14% milk solids.

Baking with Chocolate

When chocolate melts, the fat molecules are broken down by heat and liquidize. Melted chocolate provides structure and texture to the desserts it's in. Because it has a lot of fat, it tenderizes baked goods. Since dark, semi-sweet, and milk chocolates have a consistent ratio of milk solids, they provide similar textures to foods they're added to, though a higher cacao percentage will heighten flavor and also harden the dessert a bit more. Cocoa powder acts similarly to flour in a recipe, absorbing the moisture of the eggs, milk, and other liquids. If cocoa powder is in a recipe, the flour can be reduced.

Properly Melting Chocolate

Chocolate must be melted very slowly. The best way to do this is in a double boiler. You can simulate a double boiler by bringing water to a boil then reducing it to a simmer in a saucepan and putting another pan or a bowl over the simmering water. You can even use your microwave, but this must be done with great care. The recipes note this. Work in 20- or 30-second increments only, stirring after each interval. The pieces will melt at different rates, with some still melting while others are smooth already. Do not over-melt the chocolate. Stop the process when the last of the pieces are melting in with what's already hot and melted. Over-heated chocolate will seize up and harden, fracturing the recipe.

Proper Storage of Chocolate

Chocolate is a delicate substance, believe it or not—especially good chocolate. Ideally it should be stored between 55 and 65 degrees Fahrenheit. Since this temperature is hard to maintain with consistency, the recommendation is to refrigerate a chocolate confection or baked good. This hardens the chocolate, which is not the best consistency for the best flavor, as it won't melt in your mouth the way it should. When you're storing chocolate in the refrigerator—as you should—you will also need to let it sit at room temperature for a bit before serving or eating.

In the refrigerator, make sure the chocolate is in an airtight container, or wrapped in plastic wrap that's then wrapped in tin foil. Chocolate will absorb moisture from the refrigerator, causing water droplets to form on its surface. This is a break-down of sugar crystals and ruins the flavor.

Wax vs. Parchment Paper

When making bark, you need to pour the melted chocolate onto a surface from which you can lift it when it's hardened. I recommend parchment paper for this use, and the first direction is always to line a baking sheet with it. Parchment paper is coated with heat-resistant silicon. Wax paper is lined with paraffin. This is why parchment paper can be used in the oven, whereas wax paper cannot: it will melt. The temperature of melted chocolate isn't so high that it will melt the wax paper, but it's best not to even worry about it. You don't want a waxy finish on the chocolate no matter what. Another option is to use a silicon baking mat, though that will need to be washed.

Now that you know all about chocolate and how to work with it, what are you waiting for? Get barking!

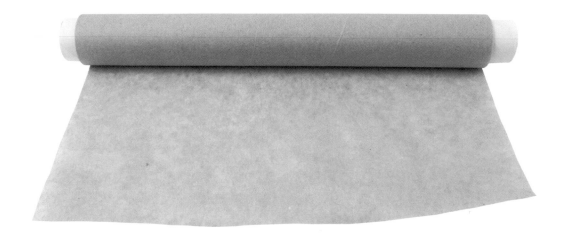

The Best Bark

There's something simply perfect about peppermint bark.
The combination of rich, smooth chocolate and refreshing,
crunchy peppermint is a match made in confectionary heaven.
It's no wonder that its introduction by the culinary-inspired
company that created it (Williams-Sonoma) was such a huge
hit, and that the now annual occurrence is so highly anticipated
across the world! Peppermint bark says *Happy Holidays*,
and when you're eating it, you get that holiday feeling like
everything is special, if even for a moment. Another part
of the joy of it is that it's so easy to make! In this chapter
you'll find 20 recipes for great peppermint
bark, from the most traditional to some very
tasty takes on the conventional.

BASIC BARK

Here's a recipe that makes what could be considered the quintessential peppermint bark—it looks and tastes like what you'd order from a fancy store for the holidays. It's so easy to make and is just delicious. The quality starts with the ingredients, so splurge on this one. Use really good chocolate, like Valrhona, Ghirardelli or Guittard, for both the dark and white chocolates. The addition of vegetable oil gives the candy the glossiness you find with the store-bought bark.

PREPARATION TIME: 45 MINUTES

12 OUNCES SEMI-SWEET CHOCOLATE, BROKEN INTO PIECES

12 OUNCES WHITE CHOCOLATE, BROKEN INTO PIECES

2 TEASPOONS VEGETABLE OIL (NO SUBSTITUTIONS)

¾ CUP CRUSHED PEPPERMINT CANDY (CANDY CANES OR STARLIGHT MINTS)

Line a cookie or baking sheet with parchment paper.

In a strong plastic bag, use a hammer or meat pounder to break the candy into shards. Put the pieces in a bowl and set aside.

Melt the semi-sweet chocolate in a double boiler, or in a bowl or saucepan set over simmering water. Alternately, put the chocolate pieces in a microwave-safe bowl and melt in 20-to-30-second increments, stirring after each one, until chocolate is just melted. You want to melt the chocolate slowly. When melted, stir in 1 teaspoon of vegetable oil.

Pour the chocolate onto the cookie sheet and use a spatula to spread it as evenly as possible over the parchment paper. Refrigerate for about 15 minutes, until set.

Next, melt the white chocolate the same way, being careful to melt it slowly and thoroughly. Add 1 teaspoon of vegetable oil when melted and incorporate thoroughly.

Pour the white chocolate over the set semi-sweet chocolate, using a spatula to spread it as evenly as possible. Sprinkle the peppermint pieces liberally and evenly over the white chocolate, pressing lightly into the layer of white chocolate.

Refrigerate for about 30 minutes, until set. Lift the candy off the parchment paper, breaking into pieces as you do. Refrigerate the bark until ready to eat.

Makes about 2 dozen pieces

WINTER WHITE
PEPPERMINT BARK

As beautiful as fresh-fallen snow, with a creamy-minty taste, this is an elegant all-white bark. Since it's just one kind of chocolate, there's no need for refrigeration between layers, so it's very easy to make, too.

PREPARATION TIME: 30 MINUTES

24 OUNCES WHITE CHOCOLATE IN BAR OR CHIPS

2 TEASPOONS WHITE CHOCOLATE LIQUEUR

¾ CUP CRUSHED PEPPERMINT CANDY (CANDY CANES OR STARLIGHT MINTS)

Line a cookie or baking sheet with parchment paper.

In a strong plastic bag, use a hammer or meat pounder to break the candy into shards. Put the pieces in a bowl and set aside.

Melt the white chocolate in a double boiler, or in a bowl or saucepan set over simmering water. Alternately, put the chocolate pieces in a microwave-safe bowl and melt in 20-to-30-second increments, stirring after each one, until chocolate is just melted. You want to melt the chocolate slowly. When melted, stir in the white chocolate liqueur, incorporating thoroughly.

Pour the chocolate onto the cookie sheet and use a spatula to spread it as evenly as possible over the parchment paper. Sprinkle the peppermint candy pieces evenly over the chocolate, pressing it in lightly in places.

Refrigerate for about 30 minutes, until set. Lift from the parchment and break into pieces. Refrigerate the bark until ready to eat.

Makes about 2 dozen pieces

BARK SEASON

At the fine culinary retailer Williams-Sonoma, where peppermint bark was developed in the late 1990s, the holiday season is a lot about bark. In fact, when bark is launched in early October, it's one of the most highly anticipated releases of the retailer's year. Stop in a Williams-Sonoma store in December, and the hallmark red-and-white packaging is everywhere. The bark has been extended to a product line that even includes peppermint bark cups. Yum!

DOUBLE-CHOCOLATE PEPPERMINT BARK

For the serious chocolate lovers on your candy list (including you!), this is a decadent bark that also features chocolate mints as its topping. Again, the better the quality of the chocolate you choose, the more flavorful and satisfying the candy.

PREPARATION TIME: 45 MINUTES

12 OUNCES DARK CHOCOLATE, BROKEN INTO PIECES

12 OUNCES MILK CHOCOLATE, BROKEN INTO PIECES

¾ CUP CRUSHED CHOCOLATE STARLIGHT MINTS

Line a cookie or baking sheet with parchment paper.

In a strong plastic bag, use a hammer or meat pounder to break the candy into shards. Put the pieces in a bowl and set aside.

Melt the dark chocolate in a double boiler, or in a bowl or saucepan set over simmering water. You want to melt the chocolate slowly. Alternately, put the chocolate pieces in a microwave-safe bowl and melt in 20-to-30-second increments, stirring after each one, until chocolate is just melted.

Pour the chocolate onto the cookie sheet and use a spatula to spread it as evenly as possible over the parchment paper. Refrigerate for about 15 minutes, until set.

Next, melt the milk chocolate the same way, being careful to melt it slowly and thoroughly.

Pour the milk chocolate over the set dark chocolate, using a spatula to spread it as evenly as possible. Sprinkle the peppermint pieces evenly over the white chocolate, pressing lightly into the layer of white chocolate.

Refrigerate for at about 30 minutes, until set. Lift the candy off the parchment paper, breaking into pieces as you do. Refrigerate the bark until ready to eat.

Makes about 2 dozen pieces

BACO-MINT BARK

With the knowledge that bacon does indeed make everything better, here's a simple but hugely satisfying bark that has bacon crumbles in every bite. It's a fabulous sweet-savory combo that's totally addicting.

PREPARATION TIME: 45 MINUTES

12 OUNCES DARK CHOCOLATE CHIPS OR BAR BROKEN INTO PIECES

4 PIECES BACON, COOKED AND CRUMBLED

1 TEASPOON BACON FAT

12 ANDES THIN MINTS, BROKEN INTO PIECES

GROUND SEA SALT

Line a baking or cookie sheet with parchment paper and set aside.

In a pan over medium-high heat, cook the bacon slices until just crispy. Place cooked pieces on a plate lined with a paper towel to soak up extra fat. Place pan to the side so cooking fat is reserved.

Place chocolate pieces in a double boiler over simmering water to melt the chocolate slowly, or place the pieces in a microwave-safe bowl and melt in 20-to-30 second increments, stirring after each, until just melted.

When chocolate is melted, add 1 teaspoon of the reserved bacon fat and stir to combine.

Break the cooked bacon pieces into small bits.

Pour chocolate onto baking sheet and use the back of a large spoon or spatula to spread it evenly in a large rectangle.

Sprinkle the still-warm chocolate with bacon bits and the Andes Thin Mint pieces. Lightly sprinkle with ground sea salt.

Refrigerate until set, about 30 minutes. Break into pieces and store in air tight container in the refrigerator.

Makes about 2 dozen pieces

MINT OREO BARK

This is a great bark to make for kids, who will delight at the sight of crumbled Oreo cookies. The bark can be broken into small pieces so it's easy to take to school or after-school activities, and be shared by a group. You'll be making multiple batches, so keep this recipe handy!

PREPARATION TIME: 45 MINUTES

12 OUNCES SEMI-SWEET CHOCOLATE, BROKEN INTO PIECES

12 OUNCES WHITE CHOCOLATE, BROKEN INTO PIECES

2 TEASPOONS VEGETABLE OIL (NO SUBSTITUTIONS)

2 CUPS MINT OREO COOKIES, BROKEN INTO BITS

Line a cookie or baking sheet with parchment paper.

Melt the semi-sweet chocolate in a double boiler, or in a bowl or saucepan set over simmering water. Alternately, put the chocolate pieces in a microwave-safe bowl and melt in 20-to-30-second increments, stirring after each one, until chocolate is just melted. You want to melt the chocolate slowly. When melted, stir in 1 teaspoon of vegetable oil.

Pour the chocolate onto the cookie sheet and use a spatula to spread it as evenly as possible over the parchment paper. Refrigerate for about 15 minutes, until set.

Next, melt the white chocolate the same way, being careful to melt it slowly and thoroughly. Add 1 teaspoon of vegetable oil when melted and incorporate thoroughly.

Pour the white chocolate over the set semi-sweet chocolate, using a spatula to spread it as evenly as possible. Sprinkle the cookie pieces liberally and evenly over the white chocolate, pressing lightly into the layer of white chocolate.

Refrigerate for about 30 minutes, until set. Lift the candy off the parchment paper, breaking into pieces as you do. Refrigerate the bark until ready to eat.

Makes about 2 dozen pieces

MOCHA JAVA BARK

An elegant bark to serve as part of a dessert tray for a dinner party or holiday gathering. The dark chocolate provides a rich base, the liqueur adds additional layers of flavor, and the peppermint "dust" is just the right amount of minty goodness.

PREPARATION TIME: 45 MINUTES

12 OUNCES DARK CHOCOLATE CHIPS

12 OUNCES MILK CHOCOLATE CHIPS

2 TEASPOONS VEGETABLE OIL (NO SUBSTITUTIONS)

1 TEASPOON DARK CHOCOLATE LIQUEUR

1 TEASPOON KAHLUA OR OTHER COFFEE LIQUEUR

⅓ CUP VERY FINELY CRUSHED PEPPERMINT CANDY

Line a cookie or baking sheet with parchment paper.

In a strong plastic bag, use a hammer or meat pounder to break the candy into shards. Put the pieces in a bowl. Using a slotted spoon, transfer the larger pieces and shards to another bowl or plastic bag. Continue to sift out the larger pieces until you have the remaining "dust," or very fine pieces of the mint candy.

Melt the dark chocolate in a double boiler, or in a bowl or saucepan set over simmering water. Alternately, put the chocolate chips in a microwave-safe bowl and melt in 20-to-30-second increments, stirring after each one, until chocolate is just melted. You want to melt the chocolate slowly. When melted, stir in 1 teaspoon of vegetable oil and the teaspoon of dark chocolate liqueur.

Pour the chocolate onto the cookie sheet and use a spatula to spread it as evenly as possible over the parchment paper. Refrigerate for about 15 minutes, until set.

Next, melt the milk chocolate the same way, being careful to melt it slowly and thoroughly. Add 1 teaspoon of vegetable oil and the teaspoon of coffee liqueur when melted and incorporate thoroughly.

Pour the milk chocolate over the set dark chocolate, using a spatula to spread it as evenly as possible. Sprinkle the peppermint dust evenly over the chocolate so that it just coats the surface.

Refrigerate for about 30 minutes, until set. Lift the candy off the parchment paper, breaking into pieces as you do. Refrigerate the bark until ready to eat.

Makes about 2 dozen pieces

THE COLORS OF CHRISTMAS BARK

Classic peppermint bark, with its layers of dark and white chocolate sprinkled with sparkly red-and-white candy cane pieces, is a beautiful sight just by itself. The addition of red-and-green-striped mint pieces and edible glitter makes this ultra-festive bark as impressive as a finely decorated Christmas tree.

PREPARATION TIME: 45 MINUTES

12 OUNCES SEMI-SWEET CHOCOLATE, BROKEN INTO PIECES

12 OUNCES WHITE CHOCOLATE, BROKEN INTO PIECES

2 TEASPOONS VEGETABLE OIL (NO SUBSTITUTIONS)

¾ CUP CRUSHED RED-AND-GREEN STRIPED PEPPERMINT CANDY

EDIBLE SILVER AND/OR GOLD GLITTER

Line a cookie or baking sheet with parchment paper.

In separate strong plastic bags, use a hammer or meat pounder to break the red and green candies into shards. Put the pieces in a bowl and stir to combine. Set aside.

Melt the semi-sweet chocolate in a double boiler, or in a bowl or saucepan set over simmering water. Alternately, put the chocolate pieces in a microwave-safe bowl and melt in 20-to-30-second increments, stirring after each one, until chocolate is just melted. You want to melt the chocolate slowly. When melted, stir in 1 teaspoon of vegetable oil.

Pour the chocolate onto the cookie sheet and use a spatula to spread it as evenly as possible over the parchment paper. Refrigerate for about 15 minutes, until set.

Next, melt the white chocolate the same way, being careful to melt it slowly and thoroughly. Add 1 teaspoon of vegetable oil when melted and incorporate thoroughly.

Pour the white chocolate over the set semi-sweet chocolate, using a spatula to spread it as evenly as possible. Sprinkle the mixed red and green peppermint pieces liberally and evenly over the white chocolate, pressing lightly into the layer of white chocolate. Next, sprinkle the bark with the edible glitter. Don't overdo it; you want the effect to be glittery, not saturated.

Refrigerate for about 30 minutes, until set. Lift the candy off the parchment paper, breaking into pieces as you do. Refrigerate the bark until ready to eat.

Makes about 2 dozen pieces

SMOTHERED BARK

Blanketing the mint pieces between the layers of chocolate creates a lovely peek-a-boo effect. It is also a little less messy to eat. Best of all, capturing two kinds of mint pieces between two kinds of chocolates is like making the world's best sandwich. The liqueur boosts the chocolatey-ness of the dark chocolate, which is always a bonus.

PREPARATION TIME: 45 MINUTES

---

12 OUNCES SEMI-SWEET CHOCOLATE, BROKEN INTO PIECES

12 OUNCES WHITE CHOCOLATE, BROKEN INTO PIECES

2 TEASPOONS VEGETABLE OIL (NO SUBSTITUTIONS)

1 TEASPOON DARK CHOCOLATE LIQUEUR (OPTIONAL)

⅓ CUP CRUSHED PEPPERMINT CANDY (CANDY CANES OR STARLIGHT MINTS)

⅓ CUP CRUSHED MELTAWAY MINTS

Line a cookie or baking sheet with parchment paper.

In separate strong plastic bags, use a hammer or meat pounder to break the candies into shards. Put the pieces in a bowl and stir to combine. Set aside.

Melt the semi-sweet chocolate in a double boiler, or in a bowl or saucepan set over simmering water. Alternately, put the chocolate pieces in a microwave-safe bowl and melt in 20-to-30-second increments, stirring after each one, until chocolate is just melted. You want to melt the chocolate slowly. When melted, stir in 1 teaspoon of vegetable oil and 1 teaspoon chocolate liqueur.

Pour the chocolate onto the cookie sheet and use a spatula to spread it as evenly as possible over the parchment paper. Sprinkle the combined mint candy pieces evenly over the dark chocolate layer, pressing them in lightly. Refrigerate for about 15 minutes, until set.

Next, melt the white chocolate the same way, being careful to melt it slowly and thoroughly. Add 1 teaspoon of vegetable oil when melted and incorporate thoroughly.

Drizzle the white chocolate over the set semi-sweet chocolate and candies, distributing it as evenly as possible.

Refrigerate for about 30 minutes, until set. Lift the candy off the parchment paper, breaking into pieces as you do. Refrigerate the bark until ready to eat.

Makes about 2 dozen pieces

HANUKKAH BARK

This beautiful white and blue bark celebrates the colors associated with the Jewish Season of Lights, but it's a striking—and delicious—combination any time.

16 OUNCES WHITE CHOCOLATE BARS (4 4-OUNCE BARS)

1 TEASPOON VEGETABLE OIL (NO SUBSTITUTIONS)

2 TEASPOONS WHITE CHOCOLATE LIQUEUR

¾ CUP CRUSHED BLUE PEPPERMINT CANDY

Line a cookie or baking sheet with parchment paper.

In a strong plastic bag, use a hammer or meat pounder to break the candy into shards. Put the pieces in a bowl and set aside.

Melt the white chocolate in a double boiler, or in a bowl or saucepan set over simmering water. Alternately, put the chocolate pieces in a microwave-safe bowl and melt in 20-to-30-second increments, stirring after each one, until chocolate is just melted. You want to melt the chocolate slowly. When melted, stir in the vegetable oil and white chocolate liqueur, incorporating thoroughly.

Pour the chocolate onto the cookie sheet and use a spatula to spread it as evenly as possible over the parchment paper. Sprinkle the peppermint candy pieces evenly over the chocolate, pressing it in lightly in places.

Refrigerate for about 30 minutes, until set. Lift from the parchment and break into pieces. Refrigerate the bark until ready to eat.

Makes about 2 dozen pieces

BARK IS BEAUTIFUL

Besides being so delicious, peppermint bark is beautiful to look at. Peppermint bark is, therefore, a perfect food for entertaining at the holidays or for special occasions like birthdays, sports team celebrations, graduations, weddings, or anniversaries.

For the best presentation, choose a dish color that will complement or offset the contrasting colors of the bark layers. For example, a cherry-red plate will complement the candy pieces on the top of the bark, whereas a pine-green plate will offset the bark's colors and help them stand out. A classic all-white plate works well, too.

Bark is also a candy that looks great in a tall stack. You can put these stacks into small, clear cellophane bags, tie them with thin red ribbons, and put them in a basket to give as party favors or gifts.

HIGHEST PEAKS
BARK

Andes Thin Mints and more chocolate?? Pass the plate! What I love about this bark is the combination of dark chocolate with the milk chocolate of the Andes mints and a blast of Rumple Mintz that will leave your mouth singing with the coolness of peppermint. A great candy to take skiing!

PREPARATION TIME: 45 MINUTES

12 OUNCES DARK CHOCOLATE (60% OR HIGHER), CHIPS OR BARS BROKEN INTO PIECES

2 TEASPOONS RUMPLE MINZ LIQUEUR

12 OUNCES MILK CHOCOLATE, CHIPS OR BARS BROKEN INTO PIECES

2 CUPS ANDES THIN MINTS, BROKEN INTO PIECES

Line a cookie or baking sheet with parchment paper.

Unwrap and break into pieces enough Andes Thin Mints to measure two cups. Set aside.

Melt the dark chocolate in a double boiler, or in a bowl or saucepan set over simmering water. You want to melt the chocolate slowly. Alternately, put the chocolate pieces in a microwave-safe bowl and melt in 20-to-30-second increments, stirring after each one, until chocolate is just melted. When melted, stir in 1 teaspoon Rumple Minz.

Pour the chocolate onto the cookie sheet and use a spatula to spread it as evenly as possible over the parchment paper. Refrigerate for about 15 minutes, until set.

Next, melt the milk chocolate the same way, being careful to melt it slowly and thoroughly. When melted, add 1 teaspoon Rumple Minz.

Pour the milk chocolate over the set dark chocolate, using a spatula to spread it as evenly as possible. Sprinkle the Thin Mint pieces evenly over the milk chocolate, pressing lightly into the layer of chocolate.

Refrigerate for at about 30 minutes, until set. Lift the candy off the parchment paper, breaking into pieces as you do. Refrigerate the bark until ready to eat.

Makes about 2 dozen pieces

DESIGNER BARK

There's something timelessly classy about black and white together. This bark, using all white chocolate with pieces of black-and-white peppermint sticks, makes for eye-catching candy. Wrapped in clear cellophane with a bright red bow, it makes an especially elegant gift.

PREPARATION TIME: 45 MINUTES

24 OUNCES WHITE CHOCOLATE IN BAR OR CHIPS

1 TEASPOON WHITE CHOCOLATE LIQUEUR

¾ CUP CRUSHED BLACK-AND-WHITE PEPPERMINT CANDY *ORDER ONLINE

Line a cookie or baking sheet with parchment paper.

In a strong plastic bag, use a hammer or meat pounder to break the candy into shards. Put the pieces in a bowl and set aside.

Melt the white chocolate in a double boiler, or in a bowl or saucepan set over simmering water. Alternately, put the chocolate pieces in a microwave-safe bowl and melt in 20-to-30-second increments, stirring after each one, until chocolate is just melted. You want to melt the chocolate slowly. When melted, stir in the white chocolate liqueur, incorporating thoroughly.

Pour the chocolate onto the cookie sheet and use a spatula to spread it as evenly as possible over the parchment paper. Sprinkle the peppermint candy pieces evenly over the chocolate, pressing it in lightly in places.

Refrigerate for about 30 minutes, until set. Lift from the parchment and break into pieces. Refrigerate the bark until ready to eat.

Makes about 2 dozen pieces

DOUBLY DECADENT DESIGNER BARK

While an all-white bark with the black-and-white mint pieces takes the prize for most elegant, this traditional double-layered bark adds a whole other layer of flavor, which is why it's named the "doubly decadent" bark. Beautiful and sooo tasty!

PREPARATION TIME: 45 MINUTES

12 OUNCES SEMI-SWEET CHOCOLATE, BROKEN INTO PIECES

12 OUNCES WHITE CHOCOLATE, BROKEN INTO PIECES

2 TEASPOONS VEGETABLE OIL (NO SUBSTITUTIONS)

¾ CUP CRUSHED BLACK-AND-WHITE PEPPERMINT CANDY (ORDER ONLINE)

Line a cookie or baking sheet with parchment paper.

In a strong plastic bag, use a hammer or meat pounder to break the candy into shards. Put the pieces in a bowl and set aside.

Melt the semi-sweet chocolate in a double boiler, or in a bowl or saucepan set over simmering water. Alternately, put the chocolate pieces in a microwave-safe bowl and melt in 20-to-30-second increments, stirring after each one, until chocolate is just melted. You want to melt the chocolate slowly. When melted, stir in 1 teaspoon of vegetable oil.

Pour the chocolate onto the cookie sheet and use a spatula to spread it as evenly as possible over the parchment paper. Refrigerate for about 15 minutes, until set.

Next, melt the white chocolate the same way, being careful to melt it slowly and thoroughly. Add 1 teaspoon of vegetable oil when melted and incorporate thoroughly.

Pour the white chocolate over the set semi-sweet chocolate, using a spatula to spread it as evenly as possible. Sprinkle the peppermint pieces liberally and evenly over the white chocolate, pressing lightly into the layer of white chocolate.

Refrigerate for about 30 minutes, until set. Lift the candy off the parchment paper, breaking into pieces as you do. Refrigerate the bark until ready to eat.

Makes about 2 dozen pieces

MINT COOKIE BARK

When it's that time of year and your cabinets and freezer are over-stocked with delicious mint cookies, transform them into this amazing bark and send it to school with your kids or bring it to your office. Be sure to save some for yourself, too. It's really good!!

12 OUNCES SEMI-SWEET CHOCOLATE, BROKEN INTO PIECES

12 OUNCES WHITE CHOCOLATE, BROKEN INTO PIECES

2 TEASPOONS VEGETABLE OIL (NO SUBSTITUTIONS)

2 CUPS MINT COOKIES (WE RECOMMEND THIN MINT® COOKIES), BROKEN INTO BITS

½ CUP PEPPERMINT CANDY, CRUSHED INTO SHARDS

Line a cookie or baking sheet with parchment paper.

Put some peppermint candies in a strong plastic bag and use a hammer or rolling pin to crush them into shards. Set aside.

Melt the semi-sweet chocolate in a double boiler, or in a bowl or saucepan set over simmering water. Alternately, put the chocolate pieces in a microwave-safe bowl and melt in 20-to-30-second increments, stirring after each one, until chocolate is just melted. You want to melt the chocolate slowly. When melted, stir in 1 teaspoon of vegetable oil.

Pour the chocolate onto the cookie sheet and use a spatula to spread it as evenly as possible over the parchment paper. Sprinkle the cookie pieces liberally and evenly over the chocolate, pressing them lightly into it. Refrigerate for about 15 minutes, until set.

Next, melt the white chocolate the same way, being careful to melt it slowly and thoroughly. Add 1 teaspoon of vegetable oil when melted and incorporate thoroughly.

Pour the white chocolate over the set semi-sweet chocolate studded with the cookies, using a spatula to spread it as evenly as possible. Sprinkle this layer with the shards of peppermint candy.

Refrigerate for about 30 minutes, until set. Lift the candy off the parchment paper, breaking into pieces as you do. Refrigerate the bark until ready to eat.

Makes about 2 dozen pieces

MINTY CARAMEL RAISIN
SEA SALT BARK

Here's an interesting bark that combines chewy raisins coated in salted caramel with dark chocolate, a sprinkling of mint, and a dash of sea salt. It's a party in your mouth.

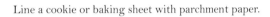

PREPARATION TIME: 50 MINUTES

12 OUNCES DARK CHOCOLATE CHIPS

1 TEASPOON CHOCOLATE LIQUEUR

½ TEASPOON VEGETABLE OIL (NO SUBSTITUTIONS)

1 7-OUNCE BAG SALTED CARAMEL COVERED RAISINS

¼ CUP PEPPERMINT CANDY, CRUSHED INTO SHARDS

SEA SALT

Line a cookie or baking sheet with parchment paper.

Put some peppermint candies in a strong plastic bag and use a hammer or rolling pin to crush them into shards. Set aside.

Melt the dark chocolate in a double boiler, or in a bowl or saucepan set over simmering water. Alternately, put the chocolate pieces in a microwave-safe bowl and melt in 20-to-30-second increments, stirring after each one, until chocolate is just melted. You want to melt the chocolate slowly. When melted, stir in the liqueur and vegetable oil.

Pour the chocolate onto the cookie sheet and use a spatula to spread it as evenly as possible over the parchment paper. Sprinkle the salted caramel raisins liberally over the chocolate, using as many as you want without overdoing it. Press them lightly into the layer of chocolate to secure them.

Sprinkle with a dusting of peppermint shards, and finish by grinding some sea salt over the bark.

Refrigerate for about 30 minutes, until set. Lift the candy off the parchment paper, breaking into pieces as you do. Refrigerate the bark until ready to eat.

Makes about 2 dozen pieces

SWEET & SALTY SURPRISE BARK

I was delighted to find bacon-flavored candy canes online. They're marketed as providing a sweet-salty surprise to those who don't know about the bacon flavoring, and it's true. Seeing the red-and-white candy, your brain thinks it's in for sweet peppermint. When the flavor is sweet bacon instead, it's a great surprise. I couldn't resist using it in a traditional bark. A light grinding of sea salt over everything enhances the flavors.

PREPARATION TIME: 45 MINUTES

12 OUNCES SEMI-SWEET CHOCOLATE, BROKEN INTO PIECES

12 OUNCES WHITE CHOCOLATE, BROKEN INTO PIECES

2 TEASPOONS VEGETABLE OIL (NO SUBSTITUTIONS)

¾ CUP CRUSHED BACON-FLAVORED CANDY CANES *ORDER ONLINE

SEA SALT

Line a cookie or baking sheet with parchment paper.

In a strong plastic bag, use a hammer or meat pounder to break the candy into shards. Put the pieces in a bowl and set aside.

Melt the semi-sweet chocolate in a double boiler, or in a bowl or saucepan set over simmering water. Alternately, put the chocolate pieces in a microwave-safe bowl and melt in 20-to-30-second increments, stirring after each one, until chocolate is just melted. You want to melt the chocolate slowly. When melted, stir in 1 teaspoon of vegetable oil.

Pour the chocolate onto the cookie sheet and use a spatula to spread it as evenly as possible over the parchment paper. Refrigerate for about 15 minutes, until set.

Next, melt the white chocolate the same way, being careful to melt it slowly and thoroughly. Add 1 teaspoon of vegetable oil when melted and incorporate thoroughly.

Pour the white chocolate over the set semi-sweet chocolate, using a spatula to spread it as evenly as possible. Sprinkle the candy pieces liberally and evenly over the white chocolate, pressing lightly into the layer of white chocolate. Finish by grinding some sea salt lightly over the bark.

Refrigerate for about 30 minutes, until set. Lift the candy off the parchment paper, breaking into pieces as you do. Refrigerate the bark until ready to eat.

Makes about 2 dozen pieces

COOKIES & CANDY BARK

Sometimes you just want it all. That's when you make this bark. It combines a little bit of a lot of yummy stuff—Oreo cookies, peppermint patties, thin mints, and crunchy candy shards.

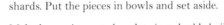

PREPARATION TIME: 60 MINUTES

12 OUNCES SEMI-SWEET CHOCOLATE, BROKEN INTO PIECES

12 OUNCES WHITE CHOCOLATE, BROKEN INTO PIECES

2 TEASPOONS VEGETABLE OIL (NO SUBSTITUTIONS)

1 8-OUNCE BAG YORK PEPPERMINT PATTY MINIS

½ CUP OREO COOKIE PIECES, CRUSHED

½ CUP ANDES THIN MINTS, BROKEN INTO SMALL PIECES

½ CUP CRUSHED PEPPERMINT CANDY (CANDY CANES OR STARLIGHT MINTS)

Line a cookie or baking sheet with parchment paper.

In separate strong plastic bags, use a hammer or meat pounder to break the cookies and candies into pieces or shards. Put the pieces in bowls and set aside.

Melt the semi-sweet chocolate in a double boiler, or in a bowl or saucepan set over simmering water. Alternately, put the chocolate pieces in a microwave-safe bowl and melt in 20-to-30-second increments, stirring after each one, until chocolate is just melted. You want to melt the chocolate slowly. When melted, stir in 1 teaspoon of vegetable oil.

Pour the chocolate onto the cookie sheet and use a spatula to spread it as evenly as possible over the parchment paper. Press mini peppermint patties into this bottom layer, but don't overdo it. Leave room for the additional cookies and candy that will go on the next layer. Refrigerate for about 15 minutes, until set.

Next, melt the white chocolate the same way, being careful to melt it slowly and thoroughly. Add 1 teaspoon of vegetable oil when melted and incorporate thoroughly.

Pour the white chocolate over the set semi-sweet chocolate, using a spatula to spread it as evenly as possible. Sprinkle the cookie and thin mint pieces liberally and evenly over the white chocolate, pressing lightly into the layer of white chocolate. Finish by sprinkling shards of peppermint candy on top.

Refrigerate for about 30 minutes, until set. Lift the candy off the parchment paper, breaking into pieces as you do. Refrigerate the bark until ready to eat.

Makes about 2 dozen pieces

PEPPERMINT POPCORN BARK

Salty, crunchy, and smothered in chocolate and mint—what could be better? Oh, that it's super easy to make? And everyone loves it? Here's another winning peppermint bark variation.

PREPARATION TIME: 50 MINUTES

1 4-OUNCE BAG POPCORN (REGULAR, BUTTER, OR KETTLE CORN)

12 OUNCES SEMI-SWEET CHOCOLATE CHIPS

12 OUNCES WHITE CHOCOLATE CHIPS

PEPPERMINT CANDIES, CRUSHED INTO SHARDS

Put candies in a strong plastic bag and use a hammer or rolling pin to crush them into shards. Set aside.

Line a baking sheet with parchment paper.

Microwave the popcorn per the instructions on the package and allow to cool.

Spread the popped corn kernels on the parchment paper, keeping it in a single layer.

In a microwave-safe bowl, melt the semi-sweet chocolate chips in 20- to 30-second increments, stirring after each, until the chips are just melted. Drizzle the melted chocolate evenly over the popcorn.

In another microwave-safe bowl, melt the white chocolate chips in the same way. When just melted, drizzle the white chocolate over the popcorn.

Sprinkle the chocolate-coated popcorn with the peppermint pieces.

Refrigerate for 30 minutes or so until chocolate sets. Break into pieces. Store in an airtight container in the refrigerator.

Makes about 2 dozen pieces

TRIPLE-LAYER PEPPERMINT BARK

If one layer of white chocolate is good, then two layers is better, right? In this recipe, the answer is a resounding "Yes!" This bark makes big, fat bites that are triple delicious!

PREPARATION TIME: 60 MINUTES

12 OUNCES SEMI-SWEET CHOCOLATE, BROKEN INTO PIECES

24 OUNCES WHITE CHOCOLATE, BROKEN INTO PIECES

1½ TEASPOONS VEGETABLE OIL (NO SUBSTITUTIONS)

1 CUP CRUSHED PEPPERMINT CANDY (CANDY CANES OR STARLIGHT MINTS)

Line a cookie or baking sheet with parchment paper.

In a strong plastic bag, use a hammer or meat pounder to break the candy into shards. Put the pieces in a bowl and set aside.

Melt 12 ounces of the white chocolate pieces in a double boiler, or in a bowl or saucepan set over simmering water. Alternately, put the chocolate pieces in a microwave-safe bowl and melt in 20-to-30-second increments, stirring after each one, until chocolate is just melted. You want to melt the chocolate slowly. When melted, stir in ½ teaspoon of vegetable oil.

Pour the white chocolate onto the cookie sheet and use a spatula to spread it as evenly as possible over the parchment paper. Refrigerate for about 15 minutes, until set.

Next, melt the semi-sweet chocolate pieces the same way, being careful to melt it slowly and thoroughly. Add ½ teaspoon of vegetable oil when melted and incorporate thoroughly.

Pour the semi-sweet chocolate over the set white chocolate, using a spatula to spread it as evenly as possible. Refrigerate these layers for about 15 minutes.

Finally, melt the last 12 ounces of the white chocolate in the same manner as the others, pouring and spreading it over the layer of semi-sweet chocolate so that there are now three layers of chocolate. Sprinkle the peppermint pieces liberally and evenly over this last layer of white chocolate, pressing lightly into the layer of white chocolate.

Refrigerate for about 30 minutes, until set. Lift the candy off the parchment paper, breaking into pieces as you do. Refrigerate the bark until ready to eat.

Makes about 2 dozen pieces

IRISH MINT BARK

This white chocolate bark is enhanced with Irish cream liqueur and looks like a field of shamrocks with green peppermint pieces on top. It's perfect for St. Patrick's Day, of course, and as a gift for an Irish friend's birthday—or for anyone who loves the color green.

PREPARATION TIME: 45 MINUTES

24 OUNCES WHITE CHOCOLATE IN BAR OR CHIPS

2 TEASPOONS IRISH CREAM LIQUEUR

1 TEASPOON VEGETABLE OIL (NO SUBSTITUTIONS)

¾ CUP CRUSHED GREEN-AND-WHITE PEPPERMINT CANDY

Line a cookie or baking sheet with parchment paper.

In a strong plastic bag, use a hammer or meat pounder to break the candy into shards. Put the pieces in a bowl and set aside.

Melt the white chocolate in a double boiler, or in a bowl or saucepan set over simmering water. Alternately, put the chocolate pieces in a microwave-safe bowl and melt in 20-to-30-second increments, stirring after each one, until chocolate is just melted. You want to melt the chocolate slowly. When melted, stir in the white chocolate liqueur and vegetable oil, incorporating thoroughly.

Pour the chocolate onto the cookie sheet and use a spatula to spread it as evenly as possible over the parchment paper. Sprinkle the peppermint candy pieces evenly over the chocolate, pressing it in lightly in places.

Refrigerate for about 30 minutes, until set. Lift from the parchment and break into pieces. Refrigerate the bark until ready to eat.

Makes about 2 dozen pieces

PEPPERMINT CANDIES

If peppermint bark is, in its elemental form, layers of chocolate studded with crushed peppermint, then any combination of these can be considered authentic (if not classic). There are 10 recipes in this chapter that play with the contents in different ways, all yielding different (and delicious) results. It's fun to play with different peppermint candies and cookies—candy canes of every color; blue "candy ice"; peppermint twists; Altoids; Lifesavers; Tic Tacs; and other breath-freshener mints; after-dinner candy mints and melt-away mints like you find at diners; Andes Thin Mints; York Peppermint Patties; Junior Mints; and cookies like Mint Oreos, Keebler Grasshoppers, and Girl Scout Thin Mints. The possibilities are limited by your imagination and tastes.

RED, WHITE & BLUE BARK

A colorful and playful bark that truly looks like a fireworks celebration when you add the edible silver sprinkles. Have more fun with it by placing toothpicks with American flags on them to the bark before refrigerating it for the final time. The bark will harden with the flags in it.

PREPARATION TIME: 60 MINUTES

24 OUNCES WHITE CHOCOLATE IN BAR OR CHIPS

2 TEASPOONS VEGETABLE OIL (NO SUBSTITUTIONS)

½ CUP CRUSHED RED-AND-WHITE PEPPERMINT CANDIES

½ CUP CRUSHED BLUE PEPPERMINT CANDIES

¼ CUP EDIBLE SILVER BALL SPRINKLES

TOOTHPICKS WITH AMERICAN FLAGS FOR DECORATION (OPTIONAL)

Line a cookie or baking sheet with parchment paper.

In a strong plastic bag, use a hammer or meat pounder to break the candy into shards. Put the pieces in a bowl and set aside.

Melt the white chocolate in a double boiler, or in a bowl or saucepan set over simmering water. Alternately, put the chocolate pieces in a microwave-safe bowl and melt in 20-to-30-second increments, stirring after each one, until chocolate is just melted. You want to melt the chocolate slowly. When melted, stir in the vegetable oil, incorporating thoroughly.

Pour the chocolate onto the cookie sheet and use a spatula to spread it as evenly as possible over the parchment paper. Sprinkle the red and blue peppermint candy pieces evenly over the chocolate, pressing it in lightly in places. Sprinkle sparingly with the edible silver ball sprinkles, just for effect. Press them lightly into the chocolate. Put the toothpicks with the flags randomly throughout the bark.

Refrigerate for about 30 minutes, until set. Lift from the parchment and break into pieces. Refrigerate the bark until ready to eat.

Makes about 2 dozen pieces

Bark Makes Other Things Better

While peppermint bark on its own can be all you need for a satisfying sweet, it's also a great addition to other recipes. This chapter explores adding peppermint bark to everything from brownies (a no-brainer) to cheesecake to pudding and even to salad! The same combination of chocolate and mint that works so well as plain bark can also send other dishes you like into another orbit. Your family and friends will be the proof of their deliciousness when the dishes disappear in their company.

PEPPERMINT BARK BROWNIES

Here's a way to have your cake and candy too! Chocolatey and chewy and layered with just the right amount of minty, crunchy goodness, these will disappear from the dessert table at your holiday gathering nearly as fast as the eggnog!

6 OUNCES SEMI-SWEET
CHOCOLATE CHIPS

8 TABLESPOONS BUTTER
(1 STICK), CUT INTO PIECES

2 LARGE EGGS

1 CUP SUGAR

1 TEASPOON VANILLA
EXTRACT

1 CUP FLOUR

½ TEASPOON BAKING
POWDER

PINCH OF SALT

1 CUP PEPPERMINT BARK
PIECES (ROUGHLY THE SIZE
OF KIDNEY BEANS
OR PECANS)

Preheat the oven to 350 degrees.

Lightly grease an 8"x8" baking dish.

In a double boiler, melt the chocolate chips and butter together slowly, stirring constantly. Transfer the mixture to a large bowl. Stir in the eggs, sugar, and vanilla. In the measuring cup with the flour, mix in the baking powder and pinch of salt. Add the flour mixture to the chocolate, stirring to blend well.

Pour the batter into the baking dish. Using your fingers, sprinkle the peppermint bark evenly over the top of the brownies.

Bake for about 30 minutes, until a knife inserted in the middle comes out clean. Be careful not to overcook. Allow to cool for 20–30 minutes before serving. Cut into small pieces.

Makes about 2 dozen small brownies

CREAMY NO-BAKE CHEESECAKE WITH CHOCOLATE BARK CRUST

It's fun and tasty to add peppermint bark to a graham cracker crust for cheesecake. Take it way over the top and decorate with some chocolate shavings and drizzled caramel.

PREPARATION TIME: 60 MINUTES + 4 HOURS REFRIGERATION

For the crust

1 ¼ CUPS CHOCOLATE GRAHAM CRACKER CRUMBS (APPROXIMATELY 14 CRACKERS)

½ CUP PEPPERMINT BARK, BROKEN INTO PEA-SIZED PIECES

¼ CUP BUTTER

For the cheesecake

1 8-OUNCE PACKAGE CREAM CHEESE, SOFTENED

1 14-OUNCE CAN SWEETENED CONDENSED MILK

1 TEASPOON GRATED LEMON PEEL

JUICE FROM 1 LEMON

1 TEASPOON VANILLA EXTRACT

Garnish (optional)

1 BAR SEMI-SWEET OR DARK CHOCOLATE

CARAMEL SAUCE

Make the crust. In a blender or food processor, pulverize the graham crackers into crumbs, working with 3 or 4 crackers at a time until all are done. Alternately, you can put the graham crackers in a strong plastic bag and crush them with a rolling pin. Put the crumbs in a bowl.

Put pieces of peppermint bark in a strong plastic bag and use a rolling pin to break them into small, pea-sized pieces. Do this until you have ½ cup. Add the bark pieces to the graham cracker crumbs and stir to combine.

Put the butter in a small, microwave-safe bowl and melt it, working in 10-second increments. Or melt it in a small saucepan. Do not overcook or burn it.

Add the melted butter to the graham cracker/bark blend and stir thoroughly to combine.

Spray a pie plate with non-stick spray, and then put the crumb mixture in it and use your fingers to press it evenly over the plate to form the crust.

Make the cheesecake. In a large bowl, beat the cream cheese until light and fluffy. Gradually beat in the sweetened condensed milk. Use a large spoon to stir in the lemon peel, lemon juice, and vanilla extract. Stir well.

Pour mixture into the prepared crust. Refrigerate for at least 4 hours.

To garnish, if desired, use a grater to grate and shave pieces of the chocolate onto the top of the cheesecake. Use a spoon to drizzle caramel over it. You can also serve the caramel on the side.

Makes 1 cheesecake, 8-10 servings

VANILLA PUDDING
À LA BARK

Small pieces of peppermint bark are a perfect topping for creamy vanilla pudding. This recipe is easy to make and tastes so much better than mixing from a box. The presentation of this dessert can transform it from something simple and straightforward to something elegant enough for a party. For a quick family dessert, serve the pudding in a large bowl from which everyone can help themselves, or do something fun like serving it in everyone's favorite mugs. Use whatever variation of bark you have on hand. For something more impressive, serve the pudding in clear wine or parfait glasses. A dollop of white whipped cream wouldn't hurt—or a fresh strawberry.

PREPARATION TIME: 60 MINUTES + 1 HOUR REFRIGERATION

2 LARGE EGG YOLKS, SLIGHTLY BEATEN

⅓ CUP SUGAR

2 TABLESPOONS CORNSTARCH

⅛ TEASPOON SALT

2 CUPS WHOLE MILK

2 TABLESPOONS BUTTER, SOFTENED

1 TEASPOON VANILLA EXTRACT

1 CUP BARK PIECES (ROUGHLY THE SIZE OF KIDNEY BEANS OR PECANS)

FRESH STRAWBERRIES (OPTIONAL)

Separate the egg yolks into a small bowl and beat them lightly.

Mix the sugar, cornstarch, and salt in a small saucepan and slowly stir in the milk. When everything is combined, begin to cook the pudding over medium high heat, stirring constantly, until it reaches a slow boil. Continue stirring while the pudding bubbles for about one minute. Remove from heat but don't turn off the burner.

Add about one-third of the hot mixture to the egg yolks, and use a whisk or a fork to combine well. Add this mixture back to the saucepan with the rest of the pudding. Return the saucepan to the heat and when a boil is reached while stirring constantly, cook for another minute. Turn off the heat and stir in the butter and vanilla extract. Allow to cool slightly.

Put the pudding in a bowl, or divide it equally among 4 dishes. Cover with plastic wrap and refrigerate. The plastic will prevent the pudding from developing a skin. After 20-30 minutes, remove, peel back the wrap, and sprinkle the tops with the bark pieces. Re-cover and refrigerate another hour or more before serving.

Makes 4 servings

BARK-LACED
ICE CREAM SANDWICHES

These are a fantastic treat on a hot summer day, and you can change up the flavors by using different ice creams. The bark on the outside definitely makes the dessert, though.

PREPARATION TIME: 45 MINUTES + 4 HOURS REFRIGERATION

2 CUPS CRUSHED PEPPERMINT BARK

1 BOX CHOCOLATE WAFER COOKIES

1 PINT VANILLA ICE CREAM, SOFTENED

Since you'll be working with ice cream, you want to have everything set up so that you can work quickly and get these into the freezer to set.

Line a small, flat baking sheet or plate that will fit into the freezer with parchment or waxed paper.

Get the ice cream out of the freezer to soften while you prepare the bark. Put pieces into a strong plastic bag and go over them with a rolling pin to create pea-sized pieces. Put the pieces in a pie plate.

Determine how many wafers will fit on the sheet (probably 6 to 8), and take twice that amount from the package. Put the sheet or plate in the freezer. You will be making one sandwich at a time and immediately transferring it to the freezer to set.

On a clean surface near the freezer, position half of the cookie pieces top down. Working one at a time, scoop out some ice cream and flatten and shape it onto a cookie then place another on top. Holding the "sandwich" together firmly but gently, roll the exposed edge through the bark pieces, or place the sandwich in the pie plate and use your fingers to put the pieces into the ice cream. Quickly put the finished sandwich on the plate in the freezer.

Continue with the other cookies, returning the ice cream to the freezer in between sandwiches if it starts to get too soft.

Keep the sandwiches in the freezer until ready to serve. If they will be in there overnight, cover with plastic wrap after about 4 hours.

Makes 6-8 sandwiches

MEGA MINTY AND CHOCOLATEY BARK-FAITS

Smooth and creamy plus rich and crunchy—a delightful combo. When layered in a decorative glass and topped with liqueur-infused whipped cream, this is a to-die-for dessert.

1 PINT CHOCOLATE ICE CREAM

1 PINT MINT CHOCOLATE CHIP ICE CREAM

2 CUPS CRUSHED PEPPERMINT BARK

1 PINT HEAVY CREAM

1 TABLESPOON CHOCOLATE LIQUEUR

1 TABLESPOON POWDERED SUGAR

Clear out some space in your freezer for the four glasses you'll use for these parfaits.

Put peppermint bark pieces in a strong plastic bag and go over them with a rolling pin to create pea-sized pieces. Transfer to a measuring cup.

Place a scoop of chocolate ice cream in the bottom of each glass. Top with a layer of crushed bark. Add a scoop of mint chocolate chip ice cream and another layer of bark. Depending on the size and shape of your glasses, continue with these layers until you've reached the top of the glass.

Put the glasses in the freezer until ready to serve.

About 10 minutes before serving, put the heavy cream in a large bowl. Whip on high until the cream stiffens. Add the chocolate liqueur and the sugar and continue beating on high until the whipped cream forms stiff peaks. Be careful not to overbeat.

Just before serving, take the glasses out of the freezer and top with the whipped cream.

Makes 4 servings

BARKY BRÛLÉE

When you take a spoonful of the creamy baked custard and get the taste of chocolate and mint to boot, you know you're in for a ramekin of pleasure!

2 TABLESPOONS UNSALTED BUTTER

6 EGG YOLKS

½ CUP SUGAR

1 TABLESPOON VANILLA EXTRACT

½ TEASPOON PEPPERMINT EXTRACT

3½ CUPS HEAVY CREAM

1 CUP PEPPERMINT BARK, BROKEN INTO PECAN-SIZED PIECES

Preheat oven to 325 degrees.

Use the butter to coat six 6-ounce ramekins. Position the ramekins in a large rimmed baking dish.

In a large bowl, whisk the egg yolks with the sugar, vanilla, and peppermint extract until they are light and lemon-colored.

Put the cream in a saucepan and heat it over medium-high heat until it just starts to boil, stirring occasionally. This will not take long. Do not let it boil.

When it's just simmering, remove from heat. Add a very little bit of the hot cream to the egg yolks, whisking hard and fast to incorporate it without cooking the eggs. Add a little bit at a time while continuing to whisk briskly. When the cream/egg blend has stabilized temperature a bit, you can begin adding more of the hot cream each time until all of it is incorporated. Distribute the custard evenly among the ramekins. Carefully place the ramekins in a roasting pan.

Using a large measuring cup, fill it with hot water and carefully pour the water around the ramekins until it reaches about half way up the sides.

Carefully put the dish in the oven and bake for about 45 minutes until the edges are firm but the center is still soft. Remove from the oven and allow to cool for about 20 minutes. Cover each ramekin with plastic wrap and refrigerate for several hours.

About 30 minutes before serving, take the ramekins out of the refrigerator and sprinkle each with the peppermint bark.

If you have a brûlée torch, use it to melt (caramelize) the top of each custard. Since the bark has chocolate in it, too, be careful not to scorch the candy. Just zap it until it's slightly melted. Put the ramekins back in the fridge to reset, about 15 minutes.

If you don't have a brûlée torch, put the broiler on high and set an oven rack on the top shelf. Put the baking dish of ramekins in the oven and leave the door slightly ajar. It won't take long for the candy to melt—about 1 to 2 minutes. Remove the tray, turn off the oven, and put the ramekins in the fridge to set.

Makes 6 servings

CRESCENT BARK ROLL-UPS

When you want to make something with kids that you know will be easy, satisfying, and delicious in the end, try this recipe. Using ready-made crescent dough feels like cheating—and tastes nothing like a true croissant—but kids love filling and rolling up the triangles, and seeing and tasting how the crescents transform during cooking. Oh, and these taste really good fresh from the oven. *Please note: Because there's already a serious shortcut involved with using the ready-made dough, be sure to buy the best brand; it's worth it.

PREPARATION TIME: 60 MINUTES

1 PACKAGE REFRIGERATED CRESCENT DINNER ROLLS

½ CUP PEPPERMINT BARK, BROKEN INTO RAISIN-SIZED PIECES

1 EGG, LIGHTLY BEATEN

Preheat oven to 350 degrees. Line a cookie sheet with parchment paper.

Put some peppermint bark in a strong plastic bag and use a rolling pin over it to break it into small pieces.

"Pop" and unwrap the refrigerated dough. Separate the triangles.

Put a scoop (about 1 tablespoon) of the bark pieces at the wide end of the triangle. Bring the dough over and roll up toward the pointed end, forming a crescent.

Put the filled crescents on the cookie sheet.

Brush the tops of the crescents with beaten egg.

Bake for 15-20 minutes until golden brown. Allow to cool before eating, but serve warm.

Makes 8 servings

PEPPERMINT PARTY CAKE

One of the added pleasures of breaking peppermint candies into shards for bark is that you discover how shiny and glass-like the candies are. They make whatever they top glittery and sparkly. This buttery yellow cake has peppermint bark pieces in the middle, but is dusted with just the shards of peppermint candy. It's a glitter cake! Serve it with sparklers for candles on the Fourth of July (or any outdoor party).

PREPARATION TIME: 2 HOURS

Cake

3¼ CUPS FLOUR

2½ TEASPOONS BAKING POWDER

1 TEASPOON SALT

¾ CUP UNSALTED BUTTER, SOFTENED

2 CUPS SUGAR

1¼ CUPS MILK, WARMED TO ROOM TEMPERATURE

2 TEASPOONS VANILLA EXTRACT

4 LARGE EGGS

Frosting

½ CUP (1 STICK) UNSALTED BUTTER, SOFTENED AND CUT INTO FOURTHS

2 CUPS CONFECTIONERS' SUGAR

1½ TEASPOONS VANILLA EXTRACT

2 TABLESPOONS WHOLE MILK AT ROOM TEMPERATURE

Topping

½ TO ¾ CUP PEPPERMINT BARK, BROKEN INTO WALNUT-SIZED PIECES OR SMALLER

5-6 STARLIGHT PEPPERMINT CANDIES

MAKE THE CAKE

Preheat oven to 350 degrees.

Lightly grease and flour two 9"x2" round cake pans.

In a bowl, whisk together the flour, baking powder, and salt. In a large bowl, beat the butter and sugar together on low speed until combined and crumbly. Add about ½ cup of the flour mixture, beating to combine, then some of the warmed milk, alternating between the dry ingredients and the milk until combined and smooth, scraping the sides and bottom of the bowl. Add the vanilla.

Next, blend in 1 egg at a time with the beaters on low, mixing until thoroughly combined. Do this with all 4 eggs. When all have been added, turn the mixer to medium and beat for another 30 seconds or so at the higher speed.

Divide the batter between the two pans, tapping the bottoms to be sure it's settled.

Bake for 25-30 minutes until the cake is golden around the edges and a toothpick inserted in the middle comes out clean. Remove from the oven and put the pans on a wire rack to cool. Allow to cool thoroughly.

MAKE THE FROSTING

Put the butter in a large bowl. Add about ½ cup of confectioners' sugar and, working with a large spoon, cream the butter and sugar together until soft and smooth. Continue to stir in the sugar ½ cup at a time until it's fully beaten in. Add the vanilla and milk and continue to stir for about 2 or 3 minutes. The frosting should be soft and creamy.

PREPARE THE TOPPING

Break the peppermint bark into pieces and set aside.

Put the mints into a strong plastic bag and use a hammer or rolling pin to break them into shards.

BUILD THE CAKE

When cool, place one of the layers on a plate. Spread about ½ cup frosting on top. Sprinkle with peppermint bark pieces, distributing evenly.

Place the other layer of cake on top of this one. Frost the sides, working from bottom to top. Frost the top last, smoothing and swirling to cover the whole cake. "Dust" the entire cake with the peppermint candy shards, using your fingers to press them in to the sides of the cake.

Cover with a cake cover or loosely with plastic wrap and refrigerate until ready to serve.

Makes 8-10 servings

BOSTON CREAM BARK PIE

This is a take on the classic Boston Cream Pie, which is actually not a pie at all, but a cake. Its creation is attributed to a chef at the Parker House Hotel in Boston, who called his pastry cream-filled sponge cake the Parker House Chocolate Cream Pie. This was in 1856. Today this is a very popular cake in diners across the United States. It is the official cake of Massachusetts. With peppermint bark "sprinkles" it becomes even more festive and delicious.

PREPARATION TIME: 2 HOURS

1 PACKAGE VANILLA PUDDING

1¼ CUPS FLOUR

1¼ TEASPOONS BAKING POWDER

¾ TEASPOON SALT

2 LARGE EGGS

2 LARGE EGG YOLKS

1¼ CUPS SUGAR

¾ CUP WHOLE MILK

2 TABLESPOONS UNSALTED BUTTER

2 TEASPOONS PURE VANILLA EXTRACT

7 TABLESPOONS HEAVY CREAM

3 OUNCES SEMI-SWEET CHOCOLATE CHIPS

½ CUP PEPPERMINT BARK, BROKEN INTO RAISIN-SIZED PIECES

Make the vanilla pudding according to the directions, allowing enough time to refrigerate and set.

Preheat oven to 350 degrees.

For the cake, spray a 9"x2" round cake pan with non-stick spray.

In a bowl, whisk together the flour, baking powder, and salt. In a large bowl, beat the eggs and egg yolks together with an electric mixer on medium for about a minute. Gradually add the sugar, continuing to beat until light and fluffy, about 3 minutes. Set aside.

In a small saucepan, combine the milk and butter and heat over medium until the milk is heated through and the butter is melted in it. Be careful not to boil the milk. When it's hot and the butter is melted, remove from heat and stir in the vanilla.

In a slow trickle, start beating the warm milk into the egg mixture with the beaters on medium. Work slowly but steadily to add all the milk. When it is thoroughly combined, use a large spoon to stir in the flour mixture about ½ cup at a time.

When the cake mix is thoroughly combined, pour it in the pan. Bake about 30–40 minutes until the cake is a golden brown color and a toothpick inserted in the middle comes out clean. Allow the cake to cool slightly before inverting onto a plate, then cool thoroughly.

For the glaze, put the chocolate pieces in a medium-sized bowl and set aside.

In a small saucepan over medium heat, bring the heavy cream to a boil, being careful not to let it boil over. Remove from heat just at the boiling point.

Pour the hot cream over the chocolate and stir until the pieces are melted. Set aside to cool while you begin to assemble the cake.

Assemble the cake. Use a long serrated knife to split the cake into 2 even layers. Put the top layer on a piece of wax paper or another plate while you work. Spread vanilla pudding on the bottom layer, distributing evenly. Place the other layer on top. Working from the center, pour the chocolate glaze on the cake. It will drip down the sides. Complete the assembly by sprinkling the peppermint bark pieces evenly over the top.

Refrigerate until ready to serve, and for at least 30 minutes.

Makes 6-8 servings

PINEAPPLE BARK BITES

Sautéing the pineapple pieces in butter enhances the flavor. The combination of dark and milk chocolates—with just a hint of cayenne—makes for a real party in your mouth.

1 RIPE PINEAPPLE

4 TABLESPOONS (¼ CUP) UNSALTED BUTTER

6 OUNCES DARK CHOCOLATE CHIPS

6 OUNCES MILK CHOCOLATE CHIPS

¼ TEASPOON CAYENNE PEPPER

5-6 STARLIGHT PEPPERMINT CANDIES

Prepare the pineapple by cutting off the top and bottom, and cutting off the tough exterior. Cut the fresh pineapple into ½-inch thick slices, using a paring knife to cut out the tough core.

Heat a cast iron or heavy-bottomed skillet over medium-high heat. Add 2 tablespoons of butter and as soon as it's melted, add several rings of pineapple. Sautee on both sides for a couple of minutes a side, and transfer to a plate. Add the additional butter and sauté the remaining slices.

Put the slices in the freezer for at least an hour. When frozen, cut the rings into 1-inch pieces.

Put the candies in a strong plastic bag and use a hammer or rolling pin to crush them into small pieces. Put in a shallow bowl.

Combine the chocolate chips in a small bowl or saucepan and heat over simmering water until just melted. Stir in the cayenne pepper.

Line a cookie sheet with parchment paper.

Using a fork, dip each pineapple piece in the chocolate, then dip in the candy pieces. Place coated pieces on the cookie sheet. When all have been dipped and coated, return to the freezer to set the chocolate, about 30 minutes. Serve.

Makes 6-8 servings

BARKED-UP PEPPERMINT PINWHEEL COOKIES

There's festive, and there's FESTIVE! Dressing up red-and-white pinwheel cookies with peppermint bark turns them into a confection that can impress even Santa Claus!

PREPARATION TIME: 2 HOURS + 6 HOURS OR MORE REFRIGERATION

1 ¼ CUPS FLOUR

¾ TEASPOON BAKING POWDER

¼ TEASPOON SALT

½ CUP (1 STICK) UNSALTED BUTTER, SOFTENED

¾ CUP SUGAR

1 EGG

½ TEASPOON VANILLA

½ TEASPOON PEPPERMINT EXTRACT

3-5 OR MORE DROPS RED FOOD COLORING

1 CUP PEPPERMINT BARK, BROKEN INTO SMALL PIECES

In a medium bowl, whisk together the flour, baking powder, and salt. Set aside.

In a large bowl, beat together the butter and sugar with an electric beater or by hand until the mixture is light and fluffy. Beat in the egg until thoroughly combined, and then add the vanilla.

On low speed or with a large spoon, stir the flour mixture into the butter/sugar mixture, working with about ½ cup flour at a time and beating or stirring until thoroughly combined.

Divide the dough in half. To prevent staining, put one half in a glass or stainless steel bowl and add the peppermint extract and food coloring. Stir to combine thoroughly.

Wrap each dough in plastic wrap, flattening out the dough into a small square or rectangle. Refrigerate for about an hour so the dough is easier to work with.

On a large flat surface, roll out the plain dough into a rectangle approximately 12"x6". Transfer to a piece of waxed paper. Repeat with the red dough, and place this on top of the other dough. Starting with a long end, roll the dough into a log, peeling off the waxed paper as you do.

When the log is formed, wrap in plenty of plastic wrap and refrigerate again until firm, at least 4 hours or up to 2 days.

Preheat oven to 350 degrees. Line a baking sheet with parchment paper.

Unwrap cookie dough and slice into ¼-inch thick rounds. Position on cookie sheet. Sprinkle with pieces of peppermint bark. Bake for 12-15 minutes until edges are browned. Transfer to wire rack to cool.

Makes about 3 dozen cookies

GLUTEN-FREE CHOCOLATE PEPPERMINT BISCOTTI

These are the perfect cookies to serve with mugs of hot chocolate after a hike or Irish coffee while wrapping gifts at night. They're crunchy and minty and perfect.

1 CUP BROWN RICE FLOUR

½ CUP UNSWEETENED COCOA POWDER

⅓ CUP POTATO STARCH

3 TABLESPOONS TAPIOCA STARCH

1 TEASPOON XANTHAN GUM

½ TEASPOON GLUTEN-FREE BAKING POWDER

¼ TEASPOON SALT

½ CUP (1 STICK) UNSALTED BUTTER

2½ CUPS CONFECTIONERS' SUGAR

2 LARGE EGGS

½ TEASPOON PEPPERMINT EXTRACT

1 3-OUNCE PACKAGE CREAM CHEESE, SOFTENED

¾ CUP PEPPERMINT BARK, BROKEN INTO PEA-SIZED PIECES

Preheat oven to 350 degrees. Line a baking sheet with parchment paper.

Make the cookies. Combine the rice flour, cocoa, potato starch, tapioca starch, xanthan gum, baking powder, and salt in a medium bowl. Whisk to combine thoroughly. Set aside.

In a large bowl, combine butter and 1¼ cups confectioners' sugar. Beat at medium speed with an electric mixer until combined, then increase to high speed and beat for another 3-4 minutes, until light and fluffy. Add the eggs and peppermint extract and beat for another minute to combine.

Slowly add the dry ingredients to the butter mixture and beat until a stiff dough forms.

Transfer the dough to the cookie sheet and form into a rectangle about 12"x3".

Bake about 40 minutes, until golden. Remove from oven and allow to cool on cookie sheet about 30 minutes.

On a cutting board, transfer the cookie and cut into slices on the diagonal using a sharp serrated knife.

Arrange pieces cut side down on the baking sheet and bake for an additional 15 minutes. Transfer cookies to a wire rack to cool completely.

Make the frosting: In a large bowl, combine the cream cheese and remaining confectioners' sugar. Beat with an electric mixer or by hand until mixture is thoroughly combined and light and fluffy.

Put the peppermint bark in a strong plastic bag and use a rolling pin to crush it into pea-sized pieces. Put the pieces on a large plate.

When the biscotti are cool, frost the long edge with the cream cheese and press into the peppermint bark pieces. Put frosted biscotti into an airtight container.

Makes about 2 dozen biscotti

SKILLET BARK-A-ROONS

If you love gooey coconut and dark chocolate—with an extra minty crunch—then you will swoon over this amazing treat. It's a little messy, but that's part of the fun.

1½ CUPS SUGAR

4 CUPS UNSWEETENED COCONUT FLAKES

4 EGG WHITES

2 TEASPOONS VANILLA EXTRACT

¼ TEASPOON SALT

1 CUP PEPPERMINT BARK, BROKEN INTO RAISIN-SIZED PIECES

Preheat oven to 350 degrees. While oven is preheating, put the cast iron skillet in it to warm up.

In a large bowl, combine the sugar, coconut, egg whites and vanilla. Stir to combine well.

When the oven is preheated, remove the skillet (with pot holders!). Put the batter into the pan and sprinkle the peppermint bark evenly over it.

Bake for 20-30 minutes until chocolate is melted on top and the edges are browned.

Allow to cool for about 30 minutes before serving. Cut into the treats in the skillet, or use a couple of large spatulas to transfer the confection to a plate where it can be sliced or broken apart to serve.

Makes about 8 wedges or a dozen "scoops"

CULINARY CREATIVITY

*When I was first learning to cook, I followed recipes religiously, thinking that if I mis-measured an ingredient or did anything out of order, that it was tantamount to botching the recipe and, in turn, the entire meal I was trying to prepare. It was years of cooking this way and consulting multiple books and magazines to read and learn about flavor combinations and cooking methods before I felt I had the hang of some things and could soften my standards. Then along came kids, and my study and contemplation time in the kitchen all but evaporated as the demand for **Food on the Table Now** took center stage. These days, I am delighted by their approach to cooking, which is so influenced by Food Network TV. Literal devourers of the program* Chopped, *where cooks must craft legitimate meals from odd ingredients in a very short amount of time, my kids have no problem experimenting. It is rare that they turn to a recipe, preferring instead to poke around in the fridge and pantry until some combination reveals itself to them. All I can say is, Bon Appétit!*

OATMEAL BARK BARS

If you're a fan of chewy oatmeal cookies, this recipe is for you. Making bars instead of cookies makes it easier to coat them with chocolate and bark, and allows you to vary the size of the treats when you cut them up and remove them from the pan. They'll soon be a family favorite!

PREPARATION TIME: 60 MINUTES

1 CUP UNCOOKED QUICK-COOKING OATS

¾ CUP FLOUR

½ TEASPOON SALT

½ TEASPOON BAKING SODA

½ CUP (1 STICK) BUTTER, SOFTENED

½ CUP PACKED DARK BROWN SUGAR

¼ CUP SUGAR

1 EGG

½ TEASPOON VANILLA EXTRACT

6 OUNCES SEMI-SWEET CHOCOLATE CHIPS

1½ CUPS PEPPERMINT BARK PIECES (RAISIN-SIZED)

Preheat oven to 350 degrees.

In a medium bowl, combine oats, flour, salt, and baking soda. Whisk to blend thoroughly.

In a large bowl, cream butter with both sugars, beating until light and fluffy, 3-4 minutes. Add the egg and vanilla and beat to combine.

Stir in the oat/flour mixture and blend thoroughly.

Spray a 9"x12" baking dish with non-stick spray and gently press the cookie dough into it. If it is too thin to get to the edges, don't press it too much. The dough should be about ¼ inch thick.

In a small microwave-safe bowl, melt the chocolate chips in 20-second increments, stirring after each, until just melted. Be careful to do this slowly. When melted and stirred, drizzle the chocolate over the oatmeal cookie dough.

Press pieces of the bark into the chocolate-covered cookie dough.

Bake for 12-15 minutes until the edge is golden. Allow to cool in the pan for about 30 minutes. Cut into squares.

Makes about 36 squares

BARK CHIP COOKIES

Pieces of peppermint bark make great "chips" for a traditional chocolate chip cookie recipe. The combination of white and dark chocolates in the bark adds a whole other layer of rich chocolate flavor.

PREPARATION TIME: 60 MINUTES

---

1 ¼ CUPS FLOUR

½ TEASPOON BAKING SODA

½ TEASPOON SALT

½ CUP (1 STICK) BUTTER, SOFTENED

½ CUP PACKED LIGHT BROWN SUGAR

¼ CUP SUGAR

1 EGG

1 TEASPOON VANILLA EXTRACT

1 CUP PEPPERMINT BARK, CRUSHED INTO PEA-SIZED PIECES

Preheat oven to 375 degrees. Line a cookie sheet with parchment paper.

In a medium bowl, whisk together flour, baking soda, and salt.

In a large bowl, combine the butter and sugars and beat on medium speed until light and fluffy. Beat in the egg and vanilla. Gradually stir in the flour mixture until well blended.

Put the peppermint bark in a strong plastic bag and use a rolling pin to crush it into pea-sized pieces.

Stir the bark pieces into the cookie dough.

Place in spoonfuls onto the cookie sheet. Bake for 12-15 minutes until lightly browned.

Transfer cookies to wire racks to cool as you continue to make batches.

Makes about 4 dozen cookies

BARK FOR ALL SEASONS

Chocolate bark has a lot going for it, maybe the best of which is that it is so easy to make. Melt chocolate(s), spread them onto a parchment paper-lined cookie sheet, sprinkle with toppings, refrigerate until set, and then—eat! Peppermint bark is synonymous with Christmas-time, but it is a great treat any time of year, as are all kinds of bark combinations. After simplicity of preparation and great flavor comes versatility in other recipes. Turns out bark is a great add-on or add-in for dessert and snack recipes throughout the year. So bark up a storm all year long!

BARKED SHORTBREAD

This is another excellent treat for the holidays, as buttery, decadent shortbread is another gift-giving tradition at this time of year. With a frosting of peppermint bark, these shortbread wedges are as fabulous as they are festive.

PREPARATION TIME: 90 MINUTES

2 CUPS FLOUR

¼ TEASPOON SALT

¼ TEASPOON BAKING POWDER

1 CUP (2 STICKS) UNSALTED BUTTER, SOFTENED

½ CUP CONFECTIONERS' SUGAR

1 TEASPOON VANILLA EXTRACT

1 4-OUNCE BAR HIGH-QUALITY WHITE CHOCOLATE

½ TO ¾ CUP PEPPERMINT BARK, BROKEN INTO RAISIN-SIZED PIECES

Preheat oven to 350 degrees.

In a medium bowl, whisk together the flour, salt, and baking powder. Set aside.

In a large bowl, beat together the butter and confectioners' sugar until light, about 3 minutes. Add the vanilla. Gradually stir in the flour mixture until dough is well combined.

Spray a 9"x2" cake pan with non-stick spray.

Press the dough into the pan, and prick the top with the tines of a fork.

Bake for 30-35 minutes until a soft golden color. Allow to cool for about 5 minutes and cut into wedges while cookies are still warm. Cool completely on a wire rack.

Put peppermint bark in a strong plastic bag and use a rolling pin to break it into raisin-sized pieces. Set aside.

When cookies are cool, put them on a large, flat dish covered with a piece of wax paper or foil.

Melt the white chocolate. Break the bar into pieces and heat slowly in a double boiler over simmering water, stirring regularly until just melted. Alternately, put the pieces in a microwave-safe bowl and heat in 20-second increments, stirring after each one, until just melted.

Drizzle the white chocolate over the shortbread cookies, and press pieces of the bark into the chocolate while it's soft. Transfer the plate to the refrigerator and allow toppings to set for 20 minutes or more.

Makes 12 cookies

CHOCOLATE MINT CAKE

This is an easy-to-make "dump" cake that's cooked in a cast iron skillet. The skillet gives the top of the cake a nice crunch and it's rich and moist enough to not need frosting. Using peppermint bark like chocolate chips gives extra flavor and texture to an already killer chocolate cake. Dollop with ice cream as suggested. Done!

PREPARATION TIME: 60 MINUTES

4 TABLESPOONS BUTTER

1 15.25-OZ BOX OF CHOCOLATE CAKE MIX

2 TABLESPOONS COCOA POWDER

1¼ CUPS WATER

½ CUP VEGETABLE OIL

6 OUNCES UNSWEETENED APPLESAUCE

4 EGGS

1 CUP PEPPERMINT BARK, CRUSHED TO PEA-SIZED PIECES

Preheat oven to 350 degrees.

In a strong plastic bag, use a rolling pin to break the peppermint bark into pea-sized pieces.

In the cast iron skillet, melt the butter over low heat. While it's melting, make the cake. (If your skillet is larger than 10.5", you'll need to reduce the baking time. Don't use a skillet smaller than 10.5".)

In a large bowl, combine the cake mix, cocoa powder, water, oil, applesauce, and eggs. Stir to combine well. Add the peppermint bark pieces and stir until evenly distributed.

When the butter in the skillet is bubbling, turn off the heat and pour the batter into it.

Bake for 35 minutes (25-30 minutes for a larger skillet) until lightly browned on the top and sides and a toothpick inserted in the middle comes out clean.

Allow to cool for about 10 minutes. The skillet will still be hot. Put a large serving plate on the counter and, working quickly and deliberately, flip the skillet so the cake is inverted onto the plate. Allow to cool slightly before serving, and add a scoop of mint chocolate chip ice cream for an over-the-top experience.

Makes 8 servings

CHOCOLATE COOKIES STUFFED WITH PEPPERMINT BARK

Slightly crunchy on the outside, fudgy in the middle, and gooey and minty in the center, these are amazing cookies that will be gobbled up by anyone who bites into one. They're great fun for kids to make, too.

PREPARATION TIME: 60 MINUTES

1 16.5-OUNCE PACKAGE CHOCOLATE FUDGE CAKE MIX

1 EGG

4 OUNCES CREAM CHEESE, SOFTENED

4 TABLESPOONS (½ STICK) BUTTER, SOFTENED

16 PIECES PEPPERMINT BARK (APPROXIMATELY 1.5"X1.5" SQUARE)

Preheat oven to 350 degrees.

Line a cookie sheet with parchment paper.

Put the cake mix, egg, cream cheese, and butter in a small bowl and beat on low with an electric mixer or by hand with a large spoon until the batter is well combined. The mixture will be very thick.

Form the batter into 16 balls, placing them on the cookie sheet as they're formed.

Using your hands, work with each ball. Flatten it, place the piece of bark on it, and squish it into the dough so that the bark gets covered completely. As each cookie is made, put it back on the cookie sheet.

When they are all formed, bake for 12 minutes until just browned on the outside.

Cool the cookies on the sheet for about 5 minutes before transferring them to a wire rack to cool completely.

Makes 16 cookies

PEPPERMINT BARK ICE CREAM

No worries if you don't have an ice cream maker—this recipe doesn't require one. The result, however, is creamy, yummy ice cream just like a churner would make. Besides being great on its own, it's also a perfect topping for brownies and cake, and a delicious filling for an ice cream sandwich made with two large cookies.

PREPARATION TIME: 30 MINUTES + 5 HOURS REFRIGERATION

2 CUPS HEAVY CREAM

1 TEASPOON PEPPERMINT EXTRACT

14 OUNCES SWEETENED CONDENSED MILK

4-5 DROPS GREEN FOOD COLORING

1 CUP PEPPERMINT BARK, CRUSHED INTO CASHEW-SIZED PIECES

In a large bowl, beat the heavy cream on high until peaks begin to form. Add the peppermint extract and continue to beat until it forms stiff peaks. On medium, beat in the sweetened condensed milk. Add the food coloring and beat until color is consistent.

Fold in the peppermint bark pieces with a spatula.

Transfer the cream to a loaf pan (8½"x4½") and put it in the freezer. Freeze for 5 hours before serving.

Makes about 1 quart (4 cups)

PEPPERMINT BARK "DIP"

Here's an easy recipe for kids to make for a party. It's a sweet "dip" for cookies of all kinds, and trust me, kids love it!

PREPARATION TIME: 15 MINUTES

4 OUNCES CREAM CHEESE, SOFTENED

1 8-OUNCE CONTAINER OF COOL WHIP

¼ CUP CRUSHED PEPPERMINT BARK PIECES

⅓ CUP MILK CHOCOLATE CHIPS

In a medium bowl, beat the cream cheese until it's light and fluffy. Stir in the Cool Whip until completely incorporated.

Add the peppermint bark pieces and chocolate chips and stir to combine.

Transfer to a bowl and put it in the middle of a plate with different cookies all around. Serve.

Makes about 1½ cups of "dip"

CHOCOLATE IS ALWAYS SPECIAL

Chocolate is as important and ubiquitous a celebratory food today as it has been for thousands of years. It's the gift you give children to delight them, the gift you give your Valentine to win them over, the gift you give your co-workers at the holidays to say "thank you," the gift you give your spouse at the end of a special dinner or occasion, and the special gift you give yourself "just because." Chocolate is fondly referred to as the "food of the gods," which is the literal translation of the Latin name for the cacao tree (Theobroma cacao). How apt! The word chocolate, however, is believed to be a derivation of the Aztec word xocoatl, which was the name of a bitter drink brewed from cacao beans. And indeed, chocolate was consumed as a bitter drink or ingredient from its presumed origins in the pre-Columbian cultures of Mesoamerica, over 2000 years BC, until the time it was shared by Montezuma with the Spanish explorer Hernando Cortes in 1519, who was repulsed by its bitterness. When honey was added to it, however, it was much more palatable to the Spaniards, and it is they who brought it back and popularized it in Europe, where it was considered a delicacy for hundreds of years. Here in America, Revolutionary War soldiers were paid in chocolate as part of their rations, it was considered so special. Cadbury and Nestle led the way in mass producing chocolate bars and treats starting in the 1800s. Today we are blessed to have so many forms of chocolate available for our pleasure, as this chapter—and this book—demonstrates. How lucky we are!!

PEPPERMINT BARK
MOUSSE AU CHOCOLAT

This is the most insane chocolate mousse you will ever make. Rich, creamy, melt-in-your-mouth, fabulous. It's as French as it gets, enough said. Topping it with peppermint bark almost seems wrong, but it certainly adds a crunch and refreshing coolness, so go ahead and Americanize it. Or have it both ways. You'll be hooked.

PREPARATION TIME: 45 MINUTES + 2 HOURS REFRIGERATION

6 EGGS, ROOM TEMPERATURE, SEPARATED

7 OUNCES SEMI-SWEET CHOCOLATE (FROM BAKING BARS, BROKEN INTO PIECES)

1 CUP PEPPERMINT BARK, CRUSHED INTO PEA-SIZED PIECES

In a large bowl, beat the egg whites with an electric beater until they form very stiff peaks. Set aside.

In a smaller bowl, whisk the egg yolks together. Set aside.

In a double boiler, or in a bowl over simmering water, melt the chocolate, stirring as it melts until just melted.

With whisk in hand, drizzle just a spoonful of hot chocolate into the egg yolks and whisk vigorously to combine. When stirred through, add just a little bit more. If you add the chocolate too fast, the egg yolks will "cook" and separate from the chocolate, so take it slow and steady. Whisk vigorously after each careful addition. As the ratio of hot chocolate to egg yolk equalizes, and the mixture is holding together, you can add a bit more chocolate at each addition. Work this way until the chocolate and egg yolks are thoroughly combined.

Fold the chocolate mixture into the egg whites until thoroughly combined.

Divide the mousse evenly into four dessert dishes or decorative glasses. Sprinkle with pieces of peppermint bark. Cover with plastic wrap and refrigerate until ready to serve, at least two hours.

Makes 4 servings

Getting Decadent with Chocolate

When I was working on this book, I started to feel like Maria Von Trapp teaching "Do-Re-Me" to the children. Why? Because in the beginning of that song, when she's teaching the children to sing, she says "Once you have these notes in your head you can sing a million different tunes by mixing them up." And that's how I feel about chocolate bark now—and as an extension, other chocolate candies. Once you get the knack of working with chocolate, you can stick almost anything in it or on it. For example, I made a bark with chocolate-covered raisins and popcorn that I called Movie Theater Bark, and Fiery Bark with hot sauce in it. Truffles are like bark in that they're a base for adding all kinds of things, and this chapter explores variations on those, too. Yes, you can make most anything with various chocolates and add-ins, just as Maria exclaimed, "You can sing most anything!"

PLAIN & PEPPERMINT TURTLES

A "turtle" is the name given to the confection combination of pecans, caramel, and chocolate. The richness of the chocolate, the gooiness of the caramel, and the chewy nutty flavor of the pecans is a home-run flavor combo. This recipe guides you through making the traditional turtle, which does not include peppermint, and a mint-dusted turtle that's extra yummy.

PREPARATION TIME: 60 MINUTES

---

8 OUNCES ROASTED, SALTED PECAN HALVES

8-10 OUNCES CARAMEL SQUARES, UNWRAPPED (JUST OVER 1 CUP)

¼ CUP HALF-AND-HALF, DIVIDED

16 OUNCES SEMI-SWEET CHOCOLATE CHIPS

4-5 STARLIGHT MINTS, CRUSHED INTO SHARDS

SEA SALT, FOR SPRINKLING

Line a baking sheet with parchment paper. Using 5-6 pieces for each turtle, make mounds of the pecan pieces on the parchment paper.

Put the unwrapped caramel pieces in a microwave-safe bowl and pour half of the half-and-half over them. Begin to melt the caramels in the microwave working in 20- to 30-second increments, stirring after each. Power to melt. It will probably take about 3-4 minutes total, but you must stop and stir the mixture every 30 seconds so you don't burn it. The first few times, stirring is almost futile but eventually the caramels soften enough to be stirred smooth. Take your time, don't overheat or heat too quickly, and keep stirring; it will come together. If the mixture seems thick and needs more cream, add the remaining amount. I used ¼ cup total and have made the recipe with both Kraft brand caramels and Werther's Baking Caramels, but caramels vary and you may need less cream than I did. The caramel is runny and loose when it first comes together, but firms up quite a bit as it cools. Alternatively, you can melt caramels on the stove over low heat, using caution and stirring frequently.

Add 1 tablespoon caramel to the top of each pecan pile.

In a medium microwave-safe bowl, add 8 ounces chocolate and heat to melt, about 1 minute on high power. Heat in 15-second increments until chocolate can be stirred smooth. I prefer working in smaller batches with chocolate and recommend doing the same and not heating all 16 ounces at once; melt additional chocolate as necessary.

Add about 2 tablespoons chocolate to the top of each pecan cluster by dolloping it on top and letting it fall down the sides. Optionally add the mints or a pinch of sea salt to each Turtle.

Allow Turtles to firm up at room temp (will take many hours) or in the fridge or freezer (about 15 minutes) before serving. Turtles will keep airtight at room temperature for weeks, or in the fridge or freezer for many months.

Makes about 12 pieces

BARKY POPCORN

Sweet and salty, cool and crunchy, fun and—yes—festive! For sure! This is a great party snack or one that will bring the family running to join you for a fireside chat-and-chow session.

PREPARATION TIME: 30 MINUTES

1 3.3-OUNCE BAG MICROWAVE POPCORN (TO YIELD ABOUT 12 CUPS OF POPPED KERNELS)

¾ CUP SEMI-SWEET CHOCOLATE CHIPS (ABOUT 6 OUNCES)

¾ CUP WHITE CHOCOLATE CHIPS (ABOUT 6 OUNCES)

¼ CUP PEPPERMINT CANDIES, CRUSHED TO SHARDS (5-6 STARLIGHT MINTS)

Make the popcorn and put it in a very large bowl.

Line a cookie sheet with a piece of parchment paper.

Put the mints into a strong plastic bag and use a hammer or rolling pin to break them into shards.

Mix the chocolate chips in a medium-sized, microwave-safe bowl. Microwave in 20-second increments until the chips just start to melt. Stir after every increment of heating. When just melted, stir in the peppermint shards. Use a spatula to scrape the chocolate out of the bowl and over the popcorn. Use a large spoon to stir the chocolate through the kernels. Work quickly as the chocolate hardens as it cools.

Transfer the candy-coated kernels to the cookie sheet and spread the mixture out. Allow to cool completely, then break apart into pieces.

Makes 6-8 servings

CHRISTMAS CRISPS

If you think chocolate-covered pretzels are yummy, wait until you try these choco-mint-chips! Yes, baked potato crisps that are dipped in chocolate and dusted with peppermint! Line them up in a cracker tray and watch them disappear!

PREPARATION TIME: 2 HOURS

2 LARGE RUSSET POTATOES

CANOLA OIL SPRAY

½ TABLESPOON SALT

6 OUNCES DARK CHOCOLATE CHIPS

6 OUNCES MILK CHOCOLATE CHIPS

5-6 STARLIGHT PEPPERMINTS, CRUSHED TO SHARDS

Preheat oven to 400 degrees.

Wash the potatoes so they are clean. Using a very sharp knife or a mandolin, slice the potatoes into very thin pieces—the thinner, the better! Put the slices in a large bowl, rinse once with cold water, then fill with cold water and let the slices soak for about 10 minutes.

Line a baking dish with paper towels and lift the slices from the bowl, shake them off, and put them on the paper towels. Pat them all dry.

Line a cookie sheet with non-stick aluminum foil. Put the slices on the foil. Spray them with the canola oil spray, sprinkle with salt, then flip them and do the same for the other side.

Bake for about 15 minutes, remove the tray, flip the slices, and bake for another 10-15 minutes, until the slices are golden and crispy. Take them out of the oven and put them on a plate to cool while you continue to make the rest.

When all the chips are cooked and cooled, line another cookie sheet with waxed paper. Put the chocolate chips in 2 small microwave-safe bowls and heat at 20-second increments, stirring after each one, until chocolate is just melted.

Dip the potato chips into the chocolate, coating some with dark chocolate and some with white chocolate. Dip the coated chips in the mint shards. Place dipped chips on the wax paper-lined cookie sheet. Refrigerate to set thoroughly, about 15 minutes.

Makes about 3 dozen chips

BARK-DIPPED BERRIES

Strawberries work best for this, but you can use large raspberries, too. Dipping fruit in chocolate is a great way to do something simple that everyone will love.

PREPARATION TIME: 30 MINUTES

1 PINT FRESH STRAWBERRIES OR LARGE RASPBERRIES (OR COMBINATION OF BOTH)

4 OUNCES SEMI-SWEET CHOCOLATE

4 OUNCES WHITE CHOCOLATE

PEPPERMINT CANDIES, CRUSHED INTO SHARDS

Put the candies in a strong plastic bag and crush with a hammer to get shards. Put in a bowl and set aside.

Line a cookie sheet with parchment paper.

Put the chocolates in a bowl and melt slowly over simmering water, swirling the chocolates gently as they melt.

Hold the strawberry by the green cap to dip it in the chocolate, then put it on the lined cookie sheet and press some candy shards into the coating. Use a long toothpick to dip the raspberries. When all the fruit has been dipped and had peppermint candy pressed into it, put the cookie sheet in the refrigerator to thoroughly set the chocolate/candy coating.

Makes about 15-20 berries

WHITE CHOCOLATE FUDGE WITH PEPPERMINT BARK

Another dessert that is as beautiful as it is flavorful. There's something so enticing about the creamy whiteness of the fudge, and the bits of bark on top are like presents under a Christmas tree.

PREPARATION TIME: 30 MINUTES + 2 HOURS REFRIGERATION

2½ CUPS (20 OUNCES) WHITE CHOCOLATE CHIPS

1 14-OUNCE CAN SWEETENED CONDENSED MILK

1 TEASPOON PEPPERMINT EXTRACT

1 CUP PEPPERMINT BAKING CHIPS

½ CUP PEPPERMINT BARK, BROKEN INTO PEA-SIZED PIECES

Line an 8"or 9" square baking pan with waxed paper.

In a double boiler or in a bowl over simmering water, melt the white chocolate chips in the sweetened condensed milk, stirring frequently. As soon as the chips are melted and the mixture is combined, remove from heat and stir in the peppermint extract and peppermint baking chips, stirring until the chips are also melted.

Pour the chocolate into the pan, spreading with a spatula to distribute it evenly. Allow to cool to room temperature.

Sprinkle with the pieces of peppermint bark. Cover and refrigerate for at least 2 hours until firm. Remove from pan by lifting up the wax paper. Cut into small squares.

Makes about 24 pieces

WHAT IS WHITE CHOCOLATE?

On the surface, white chocolate is just that: a cocoa confection that is white instead of brown. In its essence it's that, too, except that the cocoa butter doesn't contain any of the cocoa solids that make up the essential chocolate "liquor" which is the bulk of what's contained in what we think of as true chocolate. Some chocolate purists proclaim that white chocolate isn't really chocolate at all, but it does have a regulated ratio like other chocolates. It must be 20% cocoa butter and 14% milk solids (milk chocolate, as a reference, has at least 10% cocoa and 12% milk solids). Because white chocolate is rich with cocoa butter, it has the velvety mouthfeel that is associated with a great piece of chocolate.

HOMEMADE PEPPERMINT PATTIES

I have always been a huge fan of these treats, with the strong peppermint blast coated in rich dark chocolate. When I discovered it was fairly simple to make peppermint patties by hand, I've done so ever since.

PREPARATION TIME: 60 MINUTES + 90 MINUTES REFRIGERATION

2½ CUPS CONFECTIONERS' SUGAR

2 TABLESPOONS UNSALTED BUTTER, SOFTENED

2 TABLESPOONS HEAVY CREAM

1 TABLESPOON PEPPERMINT EXTRACT

12 OUNCES DARK CHOCOLATE CHIPS

In a large bowl, use a large spoon to cream together the sugar, butter, cream, and peppermint extract. The batter will be stiff. Keep at it until thoroughly combined. The consistency will be like thick cookie dough.

Working on a flat surface lined with wax or parchment paper, form the dough into a long, thin log, about the size of a quarter in diameter. Wrap in plastic wrap, twisting the ends to secure it. Put the log in the refrigerator where it will need to chill for at least an hour. Check on it as it hardens, shifting it so you don't get a flat side

When it's chilled, remove from fridge and unwrap the dough. Slice it into ¼-inch thick rounds, placing them on a platter lined with wax paper.

In a double boiler or a bowl set over simmering water, melt the chocolate chips, stirring frequently, until melted. Working one at a time, using a fork, dip each piece of dough into the chocolate to cover completely, letting excess drip off, and place back on the wax paper.

Allow the patties to set at room temperature, then refrigerate for about 30 minutes to harden.

Store in an airtight container in the refrigerator.

Makes 36 patties

CHOCOLATE PEANUT BUTTER BARK FUDGE

A luscious, layered fudge topped with pieces of dark chocolate bark. Betcha can't eat just one piece!

PREPARATION TIME: 90 MINUTES + 2 HOURS REFRIGERATION

3 CUPS SUGAR, DIVIDED

12 TABLESPOONS UNSALTED BUTTER, DIVIDED

⅔ CUP EVAPORATED MILK, DIVIDED

1 TEASPOON VANILLA, DIVIDED

1 CUP SEMI-SWEET CHOCOLATE CHIPS

½ CUP PEANUT BUTTER

1 7-OUNCE JAR MARSHMALLOW CREAM, DIVIDED

1 CUP DARK CHOCOLATE/ PEPITA BARK (P 154), BROKEN INTO SMALL PIECES

Line an 8"or 9" square pan with wax paper or foil. Set aside.

Make the chocolate fudge. In a small saucepan over medium heat, combine 1½ cups sugar, 6 tablespoons butter, and ⅓ cup evaporated milk. Bring to a boil, stirring constantly, and as soon as it looks like it's going to boil, remove from heat.

Stir in ½ teaspoon vanilla, the semi-sweet chocolate chips and about ½ cup marshmallow cream. Continue to stir until the chocolate chips are melted and everything is thoroughly combined.

Pour the chocolate mixture into the pan and distribute evenly with a spatula. Set aside to cool.

Make the peanut butter fudge. In a small saucepan over medium heat, combine the remaining 1½ cups sugar, 6 tablespoons butter, and ⅓ cup evaporated milk. Bring to a boil, stirring constantly, and as soon as it looks like it's going to boil, remove from heat.

Stir in ½ teaspoon vanilla, the peanut butter and the remaining marshmallow cream. Continue to stir until the peanut butter is melted and everything is thoroughly combined.

Pour this mixture into the pan over the chocolate layer, and distribute evenly with a spatula.

Sprinkle the chocolate bark pieces over the top, pressing lightly into the peanut butter fudge layer.

Refrigerate for several hours until set. Use the wax paper or foil to remove the fudge from the dish, and cut it into small squares.

Serve or put in an airtight container and store in the refrigerator.

Makes about 40 pieces

MOCHA FUDGE

Chocolatey and laced with coffee, this fudge hits the spot with those who like the extra kick some coffee can give to chocolate. Top with a candied espresso bean for extra crunch and goodness.

4 TEASPOONS POWDERED INSTANT COFFEE

2 TEASPOONS VANILLA EXTRACT

1 CUP CHOPPED PECANS

1 TABLESPOON KAHLUA OR COFFEE LIQUEUR

1 14-OUNCE CAN SWEETENED CONDENSED MILK

1 12-OUNCE PACKAGE SEMI-SWEET CHOCOLATE CHIPS

1 CUP (8 OUNCES) MILK CHOCOLATE CHIPS

DARK CHOCOLATE-COATED ESPRESSO BEANS FOR GARNISH

Line an 8"or 9" square pan with foil and spray lightly with non-stick spray.

In a small bowl or cup, dissolve the instant coffee in the vanilla. Set aside.

In a microwave-safe bowl, melt the chocolate chips in the microwave, working in 20- to 30-second increments, stirring after each one, until the chocolate is melted. Stir in the sweetened condensed milk until thoroughly combined, then add the liqueur and coffee/vanilla mix, stirring to combine.

Stir in the pecan pieces.

Pour the fudge into the pan and use a spatula to spread evenly. Cover with plastic wrap and refrigerate for 3 or more hours until firm. Remove by pulling out the foil.

Cut the fudge into small squares and put an espresso bean on each square. Serve or place in an airtight container and store in the refrigerator.

Makes about 3 dozen pieces

DARK CHOCOLATE PEPPERMINT TRUFFLES

Another great variation on this theme: a sublime truffle. These are the perfect confection to turn the end of a long day into something special.

PREPARATION TIME: 30 MINUTES + 4-5 HOURS REFRIGERATION

14 OUNCES SEMI-SWEET CHOCOLATE CHIPS

¾ CUP HEAVY CREAM

½ TEASPOON VANILLA EXTRACT

1½ TEASPOONS PEPPERMINT EXTRACT

2 TABLESPOONS UNSALTED BUTTER, SOFTENED

¾ CUP UNSWEETENED COCOA POWDER

In a double boiler or in a bowl over simmering water, heat chocolate chips until melted, stirring frequently.

While the chocolate is melting, heat the cream in a saucepan over medium heat until it just begins to boil, stirring frequently. As soon as bubbles faintly emerge around the edges, remove from heat and whisk in the vanilla and peppermint extracts.

Remove the melted chocolate from the double boiler. While the chocolate and cream are warm, slowly add the cream into the chocolate, stirring gently and incorporating it slowly. When they're combined, add the butter and stir it in until melted.

Cool to room temperature, and then cover with plastic wrap and refrigerate until hardened, 4–5 hours.

To make the truffles, line a large baking sheet with parchment paper. Take the chocolate out of the refrigerator and use a teaspoon to scoop it out. Roll the chocolate in your hands, forming small balls. Dust your hands lightly with cocoa powder if they get too sticky.

When the balls are formed, put the cocoa powder in a pie plate. Roll each ball in the cocoa powder and then put it back on the wax paper-lined baking sheet.

Once coated, the truffles are ready to eat. They can be stored in an airtight container in the refrigerator.

Makes about 3 dozen truffles

PEPPERMINT CRUNCH TRUFFLES

Your family and friends will be happy to see these come out after dinner! The great thing about them is their size—a perfect one-bite treat that melts in your mouth.

14 OUNCES SEMI-SWEET CHOCOLATE CHIPS

¾ CUP HEAVY CREAM

½ TEASPOON VANILLA EXTRACT

2 TABLESPOONS UNSALTED BUTTER, SOFTENED

1 CUP PEPPERMINT CANDY, CRUSHED INTO SHARDS

Put peppermint candies in a strong plastic bag and use a hammer or rolling pin to crush them into shards. Set aside.

In a double boiler or in a bowl over simmering water, heat chocolate chips until melted, stirring frequently.

While the chocolate is melting, heat the cream in a saucepan over medium heat until it just begins to boil, stirring frequently. As soon as bubbles faintly emerge around the edges, remove from heat and whisk in the vanilla and peppermint extracts.

Remove the melted chocolate from the double boiler. While the chocolate and cream are warm, slowly add the cream into the chocolate, stirring gently and incorporating it slowly. When they're combined, add the butter and stir it in until melted.

Cool to room temperature, and then cover with plastic wrap and refrigerate until hardened, 4–5 hours.

To make the truffles, line a large baking sheet with parchment paper. Take the chocolate out of the refrigerator and use a teaspoon to scoop it out. Roll the chocolate in your hands, forming small balls. Dust your hands lightly with cocoa powder if they get too sticky.

When the balls are formed, put the peppermint candy shards in a pie plate. Roll each ball in the candy and then put it back on the wax paper-lined baking sheet.

Once coated, the truffles are ready to eat. They can be stored in an airtight container in the refrigerator.

Makes about 3 dozen truffles

WHITE CHOCOLATE COCO-MINT TRUFFLES

Make these when a snow storm is forecast—they look like little snowballs, flaky with coconut and glistening with the peppermint candy shards.

PREPARATION TIME: 30 MINUTES + 4-5 HOURS REFRIGERATION

8 OUNCES WHITE CHOCOLATE BAKING BARS (GHIRARDELLI IS BEST)

⅓ CUP PLUS 2 TABLESPOONS HEAVY CREAM

1 TABLESPOON UNSALTED BUTTER, SOFTENED

1 CUP SHREDDED COCONUT (PREFERABLY UNSWEETENED)

1 CUP PEPPERMINT CANDY PIECES, CRUSHED TO SHARDS

In a strong plastic bag, use a hammer or rolling pin to crush several peppermint candy pieces into fine shards. Pour the shards onto a plate and set aside.

In a small saucepan, bring the cream to a simmer over medium heat, being careful not to let it boil. Add the butter and stir until melted. Add the white chocolate pieces, stirring constantly until completely melted and smooth.

Remove from the heat and pour the chocolate/cream mixture into a shallow bowl. Allow to cool to room temperature, then cover with plastic wrap and refrigerate until firm, at least 2 hours.

Line a baking sheet with wax or parchment paper. Use a small spoon to scoop out chocolate and use your hands to roll the scoops into balls.

Put the shredded coconut on a plate. Roll the balls in the candy shards and then in the coconut.

Serve immediately or put in an airtight container and refrigerate.

Makes about 30 one-inch truffles

WRAPPING CANDIES FOR SPECIAL GIFTS?

Homemade candies make such special gifts! They're delicious, of course, and also beautiful. The way you wrap them should let the receiver know how special they are to you (the people and the candies!). Fortunately, there are lots of options for great wrapping ideas! If you want ideas, go to Pinterest.com and look up candy wrapping. Then head to a crafts store like Michaels or Joanne's, where you'll find everything from the cellophane bags or fun containers to colored papers for tags, stamps, ribbons, and everything you need to transform your treats into beloved gifts.

PEANUT BUTTER CUPS

All-natural peanut butter gives these treats more flavor and less sugar than commercial peanut butter cups. Of course the quality of chocolate is superior, too.

PREPARATION TIME: 2 HOURS

1 CUP CREAMY ALL-NATURAL PEANUT BUTTER (I LIKE TEDDY'S)

4 TABLESPOONS (¼ CUP) UNSALTED BUTTER

¼ CUP PACKED LIGHT BROWN SUGAR

1¼ CUPS CONFECTIONERS' SUGAR

2 12-OUNCE BAGS SEMI-SWEET CHOCOLATE CHIPS

2 TEASPOONS VEGETABLE OIL (NO SUBSTITUTIONS)

Line a mini-muffin tin with paper liners and a baking sheet with parchment paper. Set both aside.

Combine the peanut butter, butter and light brown sugar in a saucepan and heat over medium, stirring frequently, until just starting to bubble. Do not overheat.

Remove from the heat and start stirring in the confectioner's sugar about ¼ cup at a time, stirring completely after each addition. When all the sugar has been stirred in, set aside and allow to cool slightly.

Place one of the bags of chocolate chips in a microwave-safe bowl and heat in 20- to 30-second increments, stirring after each one, until the chocolate is melted and smooth. Stir in 1 teaspoon vegetable oil.

Drizzle some chocolate into each of the mini muffin cups and set aside.

Scoop out about a teaspoon of the peanut butter mixture and form into a small disk, setting each on the lined baking sheet until all the batter is formed.

Refrigerate the muffin tins and the peanut butter discs for about 30 minutes so they set.

Place a disc of peanut butter into each of the chocolate-bottomed mini muffin tins.

Melt the additional bag of chocolate chips in the same way as the first, and stir in a teaspoon of vegetable oil. Top each peanut butter cup with chocolate.

Refrigerate the completed cups for another 20-30 minutes. Serve or store in an airtight container in the refrigerator.

Makes about 36 peanut butter cups

WHITE BARK WITH CRANBERRIES & PISTACHIOS

Sweet-sour dried cranberries and salted pistachios are an amazing pairing on a blanket of creamy white chocolate.

PREPARATION TIME: 45 MINUTES

24 OUNCES WHITE CHOCOLATE IN BAR OR CHIPS

¾ CUP DRIED CRANBERRIES

½ TO ¾ CUP SALTED PISTACHIO PIECES

Line a cookie or baking sheet with parchment paper.

Melt the white chocolate in a double boiler, or in a bowl or saucepan set over simmering water. Alternately, put the chocolate pieces in a microwave-safe bowl and melt in 20-to-30-second increments, stirring after each one, until chocolate is just melted. You want to melt the chocolate slowly. When melted, stir in the white chocolate liqueur, incorporating thoroughly.

Pour the chocolate onto the cookie sheet and use a spatula to spread it as evenly as possible over the parchment paper. Sprinkle the dried cranberry and pistachio pieces evenly over the chocolate, pressing them in lightly in places.

Refrigerate for about 30 minutes, until set. Lift from the parchment and break into pieces. Refrigerate the bark until ready to eat.

Makes about 2 dozen pieces

DARK CHOCOLATE BARK WITH PEPITAS & CANDIED GINGER

Another yummy sweet-salty combo: roasted pumpkin seeds (pepitas) are a crunchy, savory complement to candied ginger, which has some spiciness to it, too. The dark chocolate is a great base, but you could substitute white chocolate for a more elegant-looking bark.

························· PREPARATION TIME: 45 MINUTES ·························

12 OUNCES DARK CHOCOLATE CHIPS

1 TEASPOON CHOCOLATE LIQUEUR

½ TEASPOON VEGETABLE OIL (NO SUBSTITUTIONS)

1 CUP ROASTED, SALTED PEPITAS (SHELLED PUMPKIN SEEDS)

½ CUP CANDIED GINGER PIECES (PEA-SIZED)

Line a cookie or baking sheet with parchment paper.

Melt the dark chocolate in a double boiler, or in a bowl or saucepan set over simmering water. Alternately, put the chocolate pieces in a microwave-safe bowl and melt in 20-to-30-second increments, stirring after each one, until chocolate is just melted. You want to melt the chocolate slowly. When melted, stir in the liqueur and vegetable oil. Pour the chocolate onto the cookie sheet and use a spatula to spread it as evenly as possible over the parchment paper. Sprinkle the salted pepitas liberally over the chocolate, then with the candied ginger pieces. Press them lightly into the layer of chocolate to secure them.

Refrigerate for about 30 minutes, until set. Lift the candy off the parchment paper, breaking into pieces as you do. Refrigerate the bark until ready to eat.

Makes about 2 dozen pieces

MOVIE THEATRE BARK

What are favorite snacks at the movies? Popcorn (of course), and Raisinets (and Goobers). Here's a fantastic bark that combines both at a fraction of the cost of going to and paying for them at the movies. Who said staying home wasn't fun?

1 4-OUNCE BAG POPCORN (REGULAR OR BUTTER)

12 OUNCES SEMI-SWEET CHOCOLATE CHIPS

12 OUNCES MILK CHOCOLATE CHIPS

½ TEASPOON VEGETABLE OIL (NO SUBSTITUTIONS)

1 BOX RAISINETS (CHOCOLATE-COVERED RAISINS) OR GOOBERS (CHOCOLATE-COVERED PEANUTS)

Line a baking sheet with parchment paper.

Microwave the popcorn per the instructions on the package and allow to cool.

Spread the popped corn kernels on the parchment paper, keeping it in a single layer.

In a microwave-safe bowl, melt the semi-sweet and milk chocolate chips together in 20- to 30-second increments, stirring after each, until the chips are just melted. Stir in the vegetable oil. Drizzle the melted chocolate evenly over the popcorn.

Sprinkle the chocolate-coated popcorn with the Raisinets or Goobers pieces.

Refrigerate for 30 minutes or so until chocolate sets. Break into pieces. Store in an airtight container in the refrigerator.

Makes about 2 dozen pieces

CANDY STORE BARK

Here's a bark you can totally go to town with. Make it for an occasion that's especially candy-friendly, like Halloween or Valentine's Day. For Easter, you can use the pastel-coated candies and egg-shaped chocolates, too.

PREPARATION TIME: 45 MINUTES

1 1/2 12-OUNCE BAGS SEMI-SWEET CHOCOLATE CHIPS (18 OUNCES)

1 TEASPOON VEGETABLE OIL (NO SUBSTITUTIONS)

SELECTION OF BITE-SIZED CHOCOLATES, LIKE MINI SNICKERS, 3 MUSKETEERS, PEANUT BUTTER CUPS, PEPPERMINT PATTIES, BUTTERFINGERS, OR YOUR FAVORITE CHOCOLATE BARS BROKEN INTO PIECES

1 BAG M&MS OF YOUR CHOICE (PLAIN OR PEANUT, IN WHATEVER COLORS YOU LIKE)

Line a baking sheet with parchment paper.

Unwrap the candies and place them in a single layer on the parchment paper, distributing the different kinds evenly and randomly.

In a double boiler or over simmering water, melt the chocolate chips until just melted. Alternately, put the chips in a microwave-safe bowl and melt in 20- to 30-second increments until just melted. Pour the chocolate over the candy pieces, coating everything.

Sprinkle the top with M&Ms, pushing them lightly into the bark.

Refrigerate for 30 minutes or so until chocolate sets. Break into pieces. Store in an airtight container in the refrigerator.

Makes about 15-25 pieces

PUTTING TOGETHER A CANDY PLATE?

No matter how you store them, everyone in your house will find the stash of homemade candies, and they'll enjoy them straight out of the container. But for greater enjoyment all around—and especially for holidays, birthdays, and other special occasions when you have company—arranging candies on a special dish will definitely elicit the WOW factor. What you want to do is make the arrangement visually appealing without going overboard. The candies should be the stars of the show. You'll also want to arrange the goodies so there's some variety. When presented with the dish, your guests will get more and more excited searching for just the right ones if they're mixed up. You can create this in a few ways. Use a special plate or platter lined with one or more doilies and simply fill it with chocolates, positioning different flavors throughout the plate. Or you can use a tiered dish and put different candies on different layers of the dish for an elegant stacked effect. Again, Pinterest will give you so many great ideas to show off your candies to your family and friends.

FIREBALL CARAMEL PRETZEL BARK

All I can say about this one is Oooh La La—it's tasty and wasty with the addition of Fireball Whiskey to the caramel. Bring to an adults-only party and you will be asked to bring dessert every time!

PREPARATION TIME: 1 HOUR

MINI PRETZELS, SALTED

40 KRAFT CARAMELS, UNWRAPPED

3 TABLESPOONS FIREBALL WHISKEY

12 OUNCES SEMI-SWEET CHOCOLATE CHIPS

SEA SALT

Preheat oven to 350 degrees.

Line a baking sheet with parchment paper. Create a layer of mini pretzels on the baking sheet. Set aside.

In a microwave-safe bowl, melt the caramels in 20- to 30-second increments, stirring after each, until the caramels are just melted. Stir in the Fireball whiskey.

Pour the caramel over the pretzel pieces. Bake for 6-8 minutes until the caramel is bubbly.

Sprinkle the chocolate chips over the caramelized pretzel pieces. When they've softened, use a spoon to press, melt and smear them over the pretzels. Grind a light layer of sea salt over the bark.

Refrigerate for about 30 minutes until set, then break into pieces.

Makes 15-24 pieces

FIERY BARK

I'm a sucker for spicy foods, putting hot sauce on nearly everything. I've had to resist the urge to put cayenne pepper in many of the recipes in this book. So here, without further ado, is a bark loaded with hot stuff in a blanket of dark chocolate with some chewy dried cherries and toasted sesame seeds on top—all my favorites. Hopefully this will make your mouth sing, too.

PREPARATION TIME: 45 MINUTES

¼ CUP SESAME SEEDS, TOASTED

12 OUNCES DARK CHOCOLATE (70% CACAO), BROKEN INTO PIECES

1 TABLESPOON UNSWEETENED COCOA POWDER

2 TEASPOONS CINNAMON

1 TABLESPOON CAYENNE PEPPER

½ TEASPOON VEGETABLE OIL (NO SUBSTITUTIONS)

½ CUP ROASTED, SALTED ALMONDS, BROKEN INTO PIECES

¾ CUP DRIED CHERRIES, CUT INTO BITS

To toast the sesame seeds, heat a skillet until hot and add them. Stir and shake constantly until they just start to brown and toast. Don't overcook them. Transfer to a plate to cool.

Line a baking sheet with parchment paper. Set aside.

In a double-boiler or in a bowl over simmering water, melt the chocolate pieces, stirring frequently until just melted. Remove the bowl from above the water or off the heat, and stir in the cocoa powder, cinnamon, cayenne, vegetable oil, almond and cherry pieces. When thoroughly combined, pour onto the parchment paper and spread evenly with a spatula.

Sprinkle with toasted sesame seeds, pressing them lightly into the bark.

Refrigerate for about 30 minutes until set, then break into pieces.

Store in an airtight container in the refrigerator.

Makes 15-25 pieces

BHUJA BARK

If you're like me, you like to browse the natural foods aisle of the grocery store or go to health food stores to check out different kinds of foods. I recently discovered Bhuja snacks alongside veggie chips, quinoa crisps, and flax seed-laden crackers. The Bhuja Original Mix contains multigrain noodles, peas, peanuts, and sultanas, all crisped in a special spice blend. It's really tasty! So I layered it in chocolate and created Bhuja Bark—sweet, salty, crunchy, yummy.

PREPARATION TIME: 45 MINUTES

12 OUNCES PREMIUM WHITE CHOCOLATE, BROKEN INTO PIECES

½ TEASPOON VEGETABLE OIL (NO SUBSTITUTIONS)

1½ CUPS BHUJA ORIGINAL MIX, LIGHTLY CRUSHED

½ CUP MINI SEMI-SWEET CHOCOLATE CHIPS

SEA SALT

CAYENNE PEPPER (OPTIONAL)

In a strong plastic bag, use a rolling pin to crush the Bhuja Mix into smaller pieces. Set aside.

Line a baking sheet with parchment paper. Set aside.

In a double-boiler or in a bowl over simmering water, melt the chocolate pieces, stirring frequently until just melted. Remove the bowl from above the water or off the heat, and stir in the vegetable oil.

Pour the white chocolate onto the parchment paper and spread evenly with a spatula.

Sprinkle generously with the Bhuja Mix, pressing it into the bark. Grind sea salt lightly over the bark and, if desired, dust with some cayenne pepper.

Refrigerate for about 30 minutes until set, then break into pieces.

Store in an airtight container in the refrigerator.

Makes 15-24 pieces

BARK-BLASTED PRETZEL RODS

Making chocolate-covered pretzel sticks is a great rainy-day project for kids. While the extra topping in this recipe is crushed peppermint candies, you can use all kinds of things to coat the sticks. Try mini chocolate chips, edible sprinkles, crushed nuts, shredded coconut, other kinds of crushed hard candies, etc. Put the toppings on plates and let the kids choose.

PREPARATION TIME: 45 MINUTES

1 12-OUNCE BAG SEMI-SWEET CHOCOLATE CHIPS

1 TEASPOON VEGETABLE SHORTENING (NO SUBSTITUTIONS)

20 PRETZEL RODS

PEPPERMINT CANDIES, CRUSHED TO SHARDS

In a strong plastic bag, use a hammer or rolling pin to crush the peppermint candies into shards. Put on a flat plate and set aside.

Line a baking sheet with parchment paper. Set aside.

In a double boiler or in a bowl over simmering water, melt the chocolate chips until just melted. Alternately, put the chips in a microwave-safe bowl and melt in 20- to 30-second increments until just melted.

Dip the pretzel rods into the melted chocolate about half way, tilting bowl to easily dip. Use side of bowl to remove excess. Let cool for a minute while excess drips into bowl, then roll the stick in the candy pieces. Place the finished pretzel rods on the baking sheet.

Refrigerate for 20 minutes or until set. Store in airtight container at room temperature. Best when eaten within a few days.

Makes 20 servings

Indulgent Bark-Infused Beverages

It could be said that we saved the best for last with this chapter. There are some seriously delicious, over-the-top peppermint bark-inspired drinks here. Any or all of them would make great featured drinks at a holiday party, with festive bark-dipped rims on the martini glasses, and there are several that will warm the bodies and hearts of your ice skaters, sledders, and snowman-building outdoor enthusiasts. The chocolate-mint pairing in a beverage may be even more sublime than in a candy. It's really good. Then again, why choose? Have a bark-infused beverage with a side of bark. Cheers!

PEPPERMINT BARK CHOCOLATINIS

Here's something to drink while you're waiting for Santa to come around. He'll be happy to join the party, too! This recipe makes 2 drinks in martini glasses.

For the rims

½ CUP PEPPERMINT BARK, CRUSHED INTO SHARDS

½ CUP MILK CHOCOLATE CHIPS

For the drinks

4 OUNCES VODKA

3 OUNCES CHOCOLATE LIQUEUR

ICE

Prepare the martini glasses by doing the rims.

Put the peppermint bark shards on a saucer. Put the chocolate chips in a microwave-safe bowl and heat in 20-second increments, stirring after each, until melted. Pour the melted chocolate onto a saucer.

Dip the rim of a martini glass in the melted chocolate, turning lightly to coat. Keeping the rim facing down, dip it lightly into the peppermint bark shards. Hold the glass up for a minute or so while the candy sets onto the chocolate. Put the glass in the refrigerator to set while repeating the process with the other glass. Refrigerate the second glass.

Make the martinis. In a cocktail shaker with ice, add the vodka and chocolate liqueur. Shake vigorously. Take the glasses out of the refrigerator, shake the cocktail again, and pour into the glasses.

Makes 2 drinks

GREEN MINT-TINI

What a fun cocktail!! Color theorists say green is the color of growth, of harmony, of balance and well-being. It's the color of St. Patrick's Day (always an occasion worth celebrating). It's the color of money. It's the color of…..mint (!) a featured flavor in this beautiful and delicious cocktail. Whatever inspires you to want green, you'll love this one.

PREPARATION TIME: 30 MINUTES

½ CUP PEPPERMINT BARK, CRUSHED INTO SHARDS

½ CUP MILK CHOCOLATE CHIPS

2 OUNCES CHOCOLATE VODKA

2 OUNCES PEPPERMINT SCHNAPPS

2 OUNCES GREEN CRÈME DE MENTHE

2 OUNCES BAILEY'S IRISH CREAM

4 OUNCES ALMOND MILK

CRUSHED ICE

Prepare the martini glasses by doing the rims.

Put the peppermint bark shards on a saucer. Put the chocolate chips in a microwave-safe bowl and heat in 20-second increments, stirring after each, until melted. Pour the melted chocolate onto a saucer.

Dip the rim of a martini glass in the melted chocolate, turning lightly to coat. Keeping the rim facing down, dip it lightly into the peppermint bark shards. Hold the glass up for a minute or so while the candy sets onto the chocolate. Put the glass in the refrigerator to set while repeating the process with the other glass. Refrigerate the second glass.

Make the martinis by putting the vodka and liqueurs in a shaker half filled with crushed ice. Shake for several minutes to thoroughly combine and chill the ingredients. Strain into the bark-rimmed martini glasses and serve.

Makes 2 servings

TRIPLE CHOCO-MINT TINI

Here's another can't miss cocktail if you want one with lots of flavor and lots of sex appeal. Substitute this for dessert on Valentine's Day and your sweetheart will be swooning.

½ CUP PEPPERMINT BARK, CRUSHED

½ CUP MILK CHOCOLATE CHIPS

3 OUNCES GODIVA CHOCOLATE LIQUEUR

2 OUNCES CHOCOLATE VODKA

2 OUNCES CRÈME DE COCOA (DARK)

1 OUNCE PEPPERMINT SCHNAPPS (CLEAR)

4 OUNCES HALF-AND-HALF

CRUSHED ICE

Prepare the martini glasses by doing the rims.

Put the peppermint bark shards on a saucer. Put the chocolate chips in a microwave-safe bowl and heat in 20-second increments, stirring after each, until melted. Pour the melted chocolate onto a saucer.

Dip the rim of a martini glass in the melted chocolate, turning lightly to coat. Keeping the rim facing down, dip it lightly into the peppermint bark shards. Hold the glass up for a minute or so while the candy sets onto the chocolate. Put the glass in the refrigerator to set while repeating the process with the other glass. Refrigerate the second glass.

Make the martinis by adding the liqueurs and vodka to a cocktail shaker half filled with ice. Shake for several minutes to thoroughly combine and chill the ingredients. Strain into the bark-rimmed martini glasses and serve.

Makes 2 servings

WHIPPED CHOCOMINT-TINI

It's so fun to shop the flavored vodka section of the liquor store! There's even a whipped cream vodka. Which led to this creation, which is, admittedly, darn good.

½ CUP PEPPERMINT BARK, CRUSHED

½ CUP MILK CHOCOLATE CHIPS

2 OUNCES GODIVA CHOCOLATE LIQUEUR

2 OUNCES WHIPPED CREAM VODKA

2 OUNCES PEPPERMINT VODKA

CRUSHED ICE

Prepare the martini glasses by doing the rims.

Put the peppermint bark shards on a saucer. Put the chocolate chips in a microwave-safe bowl and heat in 20-second increments, stirring after each, until melted. Pour the melted chocolate onto a saucer.

Dip the rim of a martini glass in the melted chocolate, turning lightly to coat. Keeping the rim facing down, dip it lightly into the peppermint bark shards. Hold the glass up for a minute or so while the candy sets onto the chocolate. Put the glass in the refrigerator to set while repeating the process with the other glass. Refrigerate the second glass.

Make the martinis by adding the vodkas to a cocktail shaker half filled with ice. Shake for several minutes to thoroughly combine and chill the ingredients. Strain into the bark-rimmed martini glasses and serve.

Makes 2 servings

WHITE CHOCOLATE PEPPERMINT-TINI

The martini glass for this cocktail is laced with marshmallow sundae topping, and the rim is coated with white peppermint bark. Once the (yummy) martini is poured in, the cocktail becomes its own holiday gift—a very special treat.

PREPARATION TIME: 30 MINUTES

½ CUP WHITE PEPPERMINT BARK PIECES, CRUSHED INTO SHARDS

½ CUP MARSHMALLOW SUNDAE TOPPING

4 OUNCES VANILLA VODKA

2 OUNCES PEPPERMINT SCHNAPPS

2 OUNCES WHITE CHOCOLATE LIQUOR

CRUSHED ICE

Prepare the martini glass. Put about ¼ cup of the marshmallow sundae topping on a small plate or saucer. Put the crushed peppermint bark on a separate small plate or saucer. Dip the rim of a glass in the marshmallow and then into the peppermint bark. Use a teaspoon to drizzle additional marshmallow topping on the inside of the glass. Refrigerate until ready to add the liquid.

Make the martini. Mix the vodka, schnapps, and chocolate liqueur in a shaker filled about half way with crushed ice. Shake for a minute or so.

Line up the glasses and divide the liquid between them. Serve.

Makes 2 servings

THE MOOD FOR MARTINIS

There's just something special about a martini. It's partly the elegant glass, partly the James Bond association, partly the ubiquitous toothpick with an olive poking out from the glass announcing the drinker's distinctive preference for this clean cocktail. Today's martinis are typically made from vodka, but when they became popular—during Prohibition—they were usually made from gin, which was abundant. The strong herbal notes of gin needed to be tempered with something, which resulted in the splash of dry vermouth (infused white wine) and the olive (salty), both in extreme moderation. The cocktail was stirred in ice before being strained into a glass (shaking clouds the alcohol and further dilutes it). While it has emerged from the gin joints of Prohibition to the sleek cocktail lounges of James Bond movies, the martini is a kickin' cocktail that seems innocent and sexy on the outside but packs a punch on the inside. Especially where martinis are concerned, drink responsibly!

PEPPERMINT BARK
ICE CREAM SODAS

On a hot summer day, these are the absolute perfect mid-day snack/drink. The addition of mint to a traditional ice cream soda gives it the refreshing coolness that a hot day begs for. Keep these ingredients on hand, as you'll want to make these over and over.

PREPARATION TIME: 15 MINUTES

¾ CUP CHOCOLATE SYRUP

1 CUP MILK

4 CUPS PLAIN SELTZER
WATER, CHILLED

1 QUART MINT CHOCOLATE
CHIP ICE CREAM
(YOU'LL NEED 8 SCOOPS
FOR 4 SERVINGS)

PEPPERMINT BARK,
BROKEN INTO CHIPS

WHIPPED CREAM (OPTIONAL)

Into four glasses (preferably tall soda glasses), add 3 tablespoons chocolate syrup. To each glass add ¼ cup milk and 1 cup seltzer. Stir the contents of each glass until foamy.

Add 2 scoops of ice cream to each glass. Top with peppermint bark pieces and, if desired, dollop with whipped cream.

Drink with a straw and a spoon.

Makes 4 drinks

BARKY HOT CHOCOLATE

There are lots of mixes for hot chocolate on the grocery store shelves, but it's so much more satisfying to make real hot chocolate, and it's not hard at all. You just have to keep stirring it so it doesn't boil over and burn. It is so worth it! The other thing is that if you're going to top it with whipped cream and bark, then you want a drink that's good to the last drop. My go-to recipe for hot chocolate comes from the company that's associated with chocolate in the US: Hershey's.

PREPARATION TIME: 45 MINUTES

1 CUP PEPPERMINT BARK, CRUSHED INTO PIECES

1 CUP HEAVY CREAM, CHILLED

1 TABLESPOON SUGAR

¼ TEASPOON PEPPERMINT EXTRACT (OPTIONAL)

½ CUP SUGAR

¼ CUP HERSHEY'S COCOA

DASH SALT

⅓ CUP HOT WATER

4 CUPS WHOLE MILK

¾ TEASPOON VANILLA EXTRACT

Prepare the peppermint bark by putting pieces in a strong plastic bag and crushing them with a hammer or rolling pin. Set aside.

Make the whipped cream. Put the heavy cream in a large bowl and beat on high speed until just stiff. Add the sugar and continue beating until stiff peaks form. Stir in the peppermint extract, if desired. Put the bowl in the refrigerator while you make the hot chocolate.

In a medium saucepan, stir together sugar, cocoa and salt. Add the water and stir to combine. Cook over medium heat, stirring constantly, until mixture comes to a boil. Boil and stir for about 2 minutes. Add milk, stirring constantly, and heat to serving temperature. Do not let the mixture come to a boil.

Remove from heat and add vanilla. Make the cocoa light and foamy by beating it with a whisk for a few minutes before serving.

Pour into mugs and top with fresh whipped cream and the peppermint bark pieces.

Makes 4 servings

PEPPERMINT WHITE HOT CHOCOLATE

This is a drink as beautiful as it is tasty. It is perfect for a snowy day, or a holiday celebration. If it's an adults-only gathering, go ahead and add an ounce of anything from peppermint schnapps to white chocolate liqueur or chocolate vodka.

PREPARATION TIME: 30 MINUTES

2 CUPS WHOLE MILK

4 OUNCES WHITE CHOCOLATE, BROKEN INTO PIECES

¼ TEASPOON PEPPERMINT EXTRACT

WHIPPED CREAM

WHITE CHOCOLATE PEPPERMINT BARK, BROKEN INTO PIECES

In a saucepan on medium heat, add the milk and put in the chocolate pieces. Heat the milk slowly, stirring the chocolate pieces, until the chocolate is just melting. Stir in the peppermint extract and continue to heat until thoroughly melted and combined.

Use a whisk to beat the hot chocolate for a minute or two to make it light and foamy. Pour into mugs and top with whipped cream and the white peppermint bark pieces.

Makes 2 servings

ALL-IMPORTANT GLASSWARE

If you're going to make special drinks, be sure to give thought to the glasses—or mugs or cups—in which you want to serve them. For the martinis in this chapter, several recipes call for creating a peppermint bark rim. You'll want to use the classic clear, wide-rimmed martini glass to show off both the candy rim and the liquid inside the glass. For the hot chocolate recipes, where you want to show off the whipped cream and bark toppings, choose cups or mugs that you feel suit the occasion. For example, if you're having friends over for a dessert party, you may want to choose a fine china tea cup decorated with a pretty floral pattern. If you're just coming in from an outdoor activity and it's more casual, you may want to choose mismatched mugs, short and tall, different colors and styles. Serving the white hot chocolate in a clear glass or mug makes for a beautiful drink. As for the smoothies and milk shakes, old-fashioned soda fountain glasses can't be beat.

BARKED-UP FROZEN HOT CHOCOLATE

There's a dessert café on East 60th in New York City called Serendipity 3 that is credited with creating frozen hot chocolate. If you go there to have it, expect to wait to get in, as the café is very popular and quite small. When the treat is served, though, the wait will have been worth it. Their frozen hot chocolate is every bit as good as the real thing, and seems so much more fun. Here is how to make it at home!

PREPARATION TIME: 90 MINUTES

1¼ CUPS WHOLE MILK

½ CUP HEAVY CREAM

8 OUNCES DARK CHOCOLATE (60% COCOA), CHOPPED

1 TEASPOON VANILLA EXTRACT

⅓ CUP PEPPERMINT SCHNAPPS

2 CUPS ICE

WHIPPED CREAM FOR TOPPING

PEPPERMINT BARK, CRUSHED INTO PEA-SIZED PIECES

In a saucepan, heat the milk and cream over medium heat until just starting to boil. Do not allow to boil. Remove from heat and stir in the chocolate pieces. Stir until melted.

Allow the chocolate to cool for about 15 minutes, then stir in the vanilla extract. Refrigerate until completely cooled, about 30 minutes.

Transfer the cooled chocolate to a blender. Add the schnapps and ice. Blend on high until smooth and creamy.

Divide among 2 soda-fountain glasses. Top with whipped cream and sprinkle with peppermint bark pieces. Enjoy!

Makes 2 servings

CHOCO-MINT
SHAKE

If you and your family like thick, "chewy" shakes, then these are for you. They have all kinds of goodies in them, making them more of a dessert than a drink, but they're very fun to slurp on.

PREPARATION TIME: 20 MINUTES

2 CUPS VANILLA ICE CREAM

½ CUP MILK

4 MINT OREO COOKIES, CRUSHED

1 TABLESPOON SEMI-SWEET CHOCOLATE CHIPS

1 CANDY CANE OR 2 STARLIGHT MINTS, CRUSHED

To crush the cookies and mints without making a huge mess, use strong plastic bags to put them in, then break them up with a hammer or rolling pin. Crush them separately and set aside.

In a blender, combine the ice cream, milk, crushed cookies, and chocolate chips. Blend on high until combined. Divide into tall glasses and top with the crushed mint candy.

Makes 4 servings

PEPPERMINT MOCHA MILKSHAKES

If you're not in the mood for a simple milkshake, but you don't want to fully commit to a martini or cocktail, whip up this delicious concoction. It's a nice dessert after a long day, and it's really fun to share with a friend.

PREPARATION TIME: 20 MINUTES

1 CUP CHOCOLATE ICE CREAM

1 CUP COFFEE ICE CREAM

3 OUNCES PEPPERMINT SCHNAPPS

1 CUP MILK

CANDY CANES FOR GARNISH

In a blender, combine the ice creams, peppermint schnapps, and milk. Pulse to combine and then blend on high for a minute or so until thick and foamy.

Divide between 2 glasses and garnish with a candy cane.

Makes 2 servings

PEPPERMINT
WAKE-UP SMOOTHIE

The combination of ingredients in this smoothie may sound odd, but they come together beautifully. The flavors and textures mix and meld to yield a textured smoothie with fresh flavors and just the right pick-me-up from the coffee.

PREPARATION TIME: 20 MINUTES

½ CUP QUICK-COOKING OATS

2 BANANAS, FROZEN

1½ CUPS LOWFAT
CHOCOLATE MILK

1 CUP COLD COFFEE

½ CUP CRUSHED
PEPPERMINT BARK PIECES

In a blender, process the oats until they resemble a coarse flour.

Cut the bananas into pieces, and add them, the milk, the coffee, and the peppermint bark pieces. Pulse to get started, then process on high until everything is thoroughly combined.

Pour into 2 glasses and enjoy!

Makes 2 servings

PEPPERMINT PERK SMOOTHIE

If the wake-up smoothie was more about getting in some goodness while also getting a boost from caffeine, this smoothie—while tickled with chocolate and mint—is more about the boost from the goodness itself. You'll be amazed how the spinach, kale, avocado, and flax complement the peppermint, in particular. Really refreshing on a hot summer morning.

PREPARATION TIME: 30 MINUTES

1½ CUPS UNSWEETENED ALMOND MILK

½ AVOCADO

2 TABLESPOONS COCOA POWDER

1 TABLESPOON MAPLE SYRUP

½ CUP PACKED SPINACH LEAVES, TOUGH STEMS REMOVED

½ CUP PACKED KALE LEAVES, TOUGH STEMS REMOVED

¼ CUP PEPPERMINT LEAVES OR ½ TEASPOON PEPPERMINT EXTRACT

1 TABLESPOON FLAX SEED OIL

2 CUPS CRUSHED ICE

PEPPERMINT BARK, CRUSHED

MINT SPRIGS FOR GARNISH (IF DESIRED)

In a blender, combine the almond milk, avocado, cocoa powder, maple syrup, spinach leaves, kale leaves, and peppermint leaves (or extract). Pulse or blend on low until combined.

Add ice and blend on high until thoroughly combined and foamy.

Pour into 2 cups. Sprinkle with some peppermint bark pieces and garnish with a sprig of mint.

Makes 2 servings

PEPPERMINT MOCHA WHITE RUSSIAN

Get the movie ready, prep the bowl of popcorn, light the candles, and settle in with these amazing cocktails. Best to make a batch to have on the side for refills so you don't have to disturb the atmosphere.

PREPARATION TIME: 15 MINUTES

3 OUNCES PEPPERMINT VODKA

3 OUNCES COFFEE LIQUEUR

2 OUNCES HALF-AND-HALF

2 OUNCES VANILLA ALMOND MILK

PEPPERMINT BARK, CRUSHED

Fill 2 cocktail glasses half full with crushed ice.

Pour 1.5 ounces of vodka and coffee liqueur into each. Add 1 ounce each half-and-half and vanilla almond milk. Stir.

Garnish with pieces of peppermint bark.

Makes 2 servings

THE PHENOMENON OF FLAVORED VODKAS

It used to be that a well-stocked bar included a bottle each of the basics: vodka, gin, rum, tequila, whiskey, scotch, and brandy. Mixers were ice, tonic, some sodas, fruit juices, maybe olives, cocktail onions, or maraschino cherries. Today this selection is dated and boring. Of course you should have all the basics so you can please all your guests, but there are so many more interesting options to stock your bar with, flavors that can be combined in all kinds of ways. While the likes of flavors as varied as whipped cream, cherry, lemon, chocolate, vanilla, peppermint, sour apple, black currant, pomegranate, passion fruit, jalapeño pepper and many more, seems modern, it turns out that back in the mid to late 1700s vodkas were being "aromatized" with the popular flavors of the day, including ginger, calendula, birch, horseradish, dill, cherry, raspberry, and even watermelon. So flavored vodkas aren't as "modern" as we think. But certainly today's flavors reflect people's tastes for the sweet, spicy, and fruity more than the herbed or aromatic of another era. They certainly work for some of the drinks in this chapter!

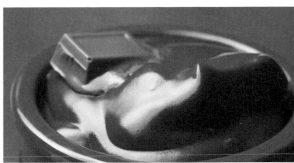

INDEX

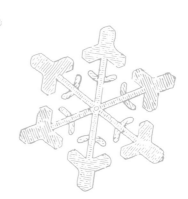

Acknowledgements

I would like to thank John Whalen and his exceptional team at Cider Mill Press—Alex Lewis, Brittany Wason, Kelly Gauthier, Alicia Freile, and Cindy Katz—for giving me the opportunity to write this book full of super-yummy recipes, and for making it look so, so good! It is a privilege to work with all of you.

About the Author

Dominique DeVito has written several cookbooks, most recently *The Cast-Iron Baking Book* for Cider Mill Press. Making—and eating—the bark recipes in this book was a very special treat that the whole family enjoyed. Dominique is an owner of the Hudson-Chatham Winery in Ghent, NY, where good wine, good food, and rural living make for a good life.

About Cider Mill Press
Book Publishers

Good ideas ripen with time. From seed to harvest, Cider Mill Press brings fine reading, information, and entertainment together between the covers of its creatively crafted books. Our Cider Mill bears fruit twice a year, publishing a new crop of titles each spring and fall.

"Where Good Books Are Ready for Press"

Visit us on the Web at
www.cidermillpress.com
or write to us at
PO Box 454
Kennebunkport, Maine 04046